TOP AI BUSINESS IDEAS

AN AI BOOK EXPOSING THE GOLDMINES YOU HAVE BEEN FINDING

By

ANDREW MARK

Copyright @ 2023 Andrew Mark
All rights reserved.

No part of this book may be reproduced, distributed or transmitted in any form or by any means, including photocopying, recording or other electronic or mechanical methods, without prior written permission of the publisher, except in the case of brief quotations embodied in critical reviews and certain non-commercial uses permitted by copyright law.

TABLE OF CONTENTS

TOP AI BUSINESS IDEAS 1
INTRODUCTION 4
CHAPTER ONE 10
    THE AI REVOLUTION IN BUSINESS 10
CHAPTER TWO 18
    NAVIGATING THE AI LANDSCAPE 18
CHAPTER THREE 32
    ETHICAL AND LEGAL CONSIDERATIONS IN AI BUSINESS 32
CHAPTER FOUR 42
    AI IN AGRICULTURE: GROWING BEYOND LIMITS 42
CHAPTER FIVE 52
    REVOLUTIONIZING HEALTHCARE WITH AI 52
CHAPTER SIX 62
    AI-POWERED RETAIL: FROM BRICK-AND-MORTAR TO CLICK-AND-COLLECT 62
CHAPTER SEVEN 72
    AI IN REAL ESTATE: THE SMART PROPERTY SHIFT 72
CHAPTER EIGHT 80
    AI-DRIVEN FINANCE: FROM BANKING TO WEALTH MANAGEMENT 80
CHAPTER NINE 90
    SMART CITIES: AI-POWERED URBAN INNOVATION 90
CHAPTER TEN 98
    AI IN EDUCATION: SHAPING THE FUTURE OF LEARNING 98
CHAPTER ELEVEN 106
    AI IN ENTERTAINMENT: CRAFTING PERSONALIZED EXPERIENCES 106
CHAPTER TWELVE 114

AI AND SUSTAINABILITY: GREENING THE BUSINESS WORLD 114

CHAPTER THIRTEEN 124

    STARTING YOUR AI BUSINESS: FROM IDEA TO IMPLEMENTATION 124

CHAPTER FOURTEEN 134

    FUNDING YOUR AI VENTURE: INVESTORS AND OPPORTUNITIES 134

CHAPTER FIFTEEN 142

    AI BUSINESS STRATEGIES: MARKETING, SCALING, AND MONETIZATION 142

CHAPTER SIXTEEN 152

    AI BUSINESS SUCCESS STORIES..............152

CHAPTER SEVENTEEN..............198

    AI BUSINESS FAILURES: LESSONS TO LEARN FROM..............198

APPENDIX 214

    RESOURCES FOR ASPIRING AI ENTREPRENEURS 214

        I. UNDERSTANDING AI TOOLS AND FRAMEWORKS 223

        II. REAL-WORLD APPLICATIONS 225

        III. STATISTICS SHOWCASING IMPACT..............228

        IV. CHALLENGES AND FUTURE DIRECTIONS 229

Andrew Mark

INTRODUCTION

In the hushed corridors of the tech industry, a revolution is underway—a revolution driven by artificial intelligence, the technological Prometheus of our age. It is a revolution that promises to reshape the very foundations of business, to ignite innovation, and to send shockwaves through the global economy. The dawn of AI is upon us, and it is dazzling, audacious, and limitless in its potential.

Picture this: in the sprawling metropolis of tomorrow, a multitude of industries converge, each transformed by the wizardry of machine learning, data analytics, and neural networks. Autonomous vehicles snake through city streets, making traffic jams a relic of the past. A medical diagnosis arrives in seconds, with the precision of the most skilled human physician. The grocery store knows your preferences before you do, ensuring your favorite snack is always in stock. This is not science fiction; this is the extraordinary reality that AI is shaping.

Top AI Business Ideas is a journey into this new reality, an exploration of the boundless opportunities, and the profound challenges that AI presents to businesses of all sizes. It is a call to arms for the innovators, the dreamers, the disruptors who recognize that in this brave new world, the key to success is the mastery of artificial intelligence.

AI, once a monolithic concept that seemed fit only for the greatest minds of our time, has evolved into a practical and transformative tool that can catapult your business to uncharted heights. Whether you are a startup striving for that initial breakthrough, a traditional business grappling with digital transformation, or a seasoned tech giant looking to stay ahead of the curve, AI is your ticket to unlock the future.

This book will serve as your guide—a lighthouse amidst the fog of complex algorithms and jargon. It will reveal how AI can enhance customer experiences, optimize operations, and create new revenue streams. It will unveil the stories of pioneers who, armed with AI, have reinvented their industries and emerged as titans. It will equip you with insights into the ethical considerations, ensuring you tread the path of innovation responsibly and sustainably.

But this journey is not a mere spectator sport. It is a call to action. You will be encouraged not only to learn but to practice, not only to understand but to implement. AI is a craft, an art, a science, and you are invited to be the artist, the explorer, the scientist.

We invite you to step into the exhilarating realm of Top AI Business Ideas. Prepare to be stunned and moved, but most importantly, prepare to be empowered. For AI is not just a tool—it is the master key that unlocks the door to a future where the unimaginable becomes attainable. The future belongs to those who dare to grasp it. Will you be one of them?

Part I: Laying the Foundation

CHAPTER ONE

THE AI REVOLUTION IN BUSINESS

The dawn of the 21st century has witnessed an unprecedented transformation in the business environment, driven by the relentless advance of Artificial Intelligence (AI) technologies. This chapter delves into the phenomenon of the AI revolution in business, exploring its origins, evolution, and the profound effect it has had on organizations across the world. As businesses deal with the growing complexities of the digital age, AI emerges as a critical force that promises to reshape the very fabric of commerce.

The Genesis of the AI Revolution

To understand the AI revolution, it is important to trace its roots back to the mid-20th century. The word "Artificial Intelligence" was first coined in 1956, signifying a novel frontier in computing where machines could replicate human cognitive functions. However, it was only in recent decades that AI technologies advanced to a point where they could be practically applied in business settings.

The Evolving Landscape

As the capabilities of AI grew, so too did its applicability in various business domains. Early adopters primarily came from industries like finance, where predictive analytics and algorithmic trading algorithms were put into play. In healthcare, AI began to help with diagnostics and drug discovery, while e-commerce companies harnessed it for customer personalization and recommendation systems.

One of the defining times that propelled AI into the business mainstream was the rise of the "Big Data" era. The exponential growth of data gathering and storage capabilities, combined with the increased computational power of machines, set the stage for AI's rapid expansion. Companies started understanding that the data they were accumulating could be transformed into actionable insights and automated decision-making processes.

The Impact on Business Operations

The proliferation of AI has significantly altered the way businesses work. The following sections describe key areas where AI has revolutionized business practices.

Data-Driven Decision Making

AI enables businesses to sift through vast datasets and extract valuable insights that might have otherwise stayed hidden. Advanced analytics, machine learning, and predictive modeling tools enable organizations to make data-driven decisions that optimize operations, reduce costs, and drive revenue growth.

For example, retail companies can utilize AI to predict demand, adjusting inventory levels in real time to avoid overstock or stockouts. In supply chain management, AI-driven logistics solutions optimize routes and predict maintenance needs, reducing transportation costs and improving efficiency.

Customer Experience Enhancement

The age of AI has seen an unprecedented shift towards personalized customer experiences. Chatbots, virtual assistants, and recommendation engines driven by AI analyze customer behavior and preferences to tailor product offerings, deliver personalized marketing campaigns, and provide round-the-clock customer support.

E-commerce platforms, for instance, leverage AI to offer customers product recommendations based on their browsing and buy history. This level of personalization not only enhances customer happiness but also boosts sales and customer loyalty.

Automation and Efficiency

AI-driven automation has the ability to revolutionize business processes. Repetitive, rule-based tasks can be handed over to AI, freeing up human resources for more strategic, creative, and complex projects. This not only reduces labor costs but also minimizes errors and enhances total efficiency.

In manufacturing, AI-driven robots and automated systems optimize production lines, reducing defects and increasing output. In the financial business, AI-powered algorithms execute high-frequency trades with unmatched precision and speed.

Risk Mitigation

AI's ability to examine vast datasets in real-time has been instrumental in risk mitigation. For banks and insurance companies, AI is used to identify fraudulent activities and assess credit risk. In cybersecurity, AI-driven solutions constantly watch network data for anomalous patterns, helping to thwart cyberattacks.

Innovation and New Business Models

AI has spurred the development of totally new business models and industries. For instance, the rise of ride-sharing services like Uber and Lyft was made possible through AI-powered matching algorithms. Likewise, the field of autonomous vehicles is rapidly changing, with AI serving as the core technology for self-driving cars.

The Challenges of the AI Revolution

While the AI revolution offers immense potential, it is not without challenges. Businesses must deal with ethical concerns, data privacy, regulatory issues, and the displacement of jobs due to automation. Ensuring that AI is used ethically and responsibly is a critical necessity.

The AI revolution in business is not a futuristic vision; it is the fact of the present. Organizations across industries are harnessing AI's power to make better decisions, improve customer experiences, automate processes, mitigate risks, and drive innovation. The evolution of AI in business is a dynamic and ongoing process, and keeping competitive now requires not just understanding AI but effectively integrating it into the fabric of the company. This book will explore the many facets of the AI revolution, offering insights, strategies, and practical advice for businesses seeking to thrive in this transformative era.

CHAPTER TWO

NAVIGATING THE AI LANDSCAPE

The field of Artificial Intelligence (AI) is rapidly evolving, revolutionizing various sectors, including healthcare, finance, transportation, and more. Navigating the AI landscape requires a comprehensive understanding of its concepts, challenges, and opportunities. In this chapter, we will delve into the practical aspects of AI, exploring its types, applications, and ethical considerations.

Types of AI:

AI can be broadly classified into three categories: narrow AI, general AI, and super-intelligent AI. Narrow AI, also known as weak AI, is designed to perform specific tasks and is prevalent in applications like voice assistants and recommendation systems. General AI refers to an AI system that possesses human-like intelligence across a wide range of tasks. Super-intelligent AI surpasses human intelligence and is a topic of speculation and research.

Applications of AI:

AI has found applications in diverse fields. In healthcare, it aids in diagnosis, drug discovery, and personalized medicine. In finance, AI algorithms analyze market trends, automate trading, and detect fraudulent activities. Furthermore, AI has facilitated advancements in autonomous vehicles, natural language processing, virtual assistants, and more. Understanding these applications can help individuals and organizations leverage AI for their specific needs.

Ethical Considerations:

As AI continues to advance, ethical considerations become increasingly important. Bias in AI algorithms, privacy concerns, and job displacement are some of the ethical issues associated with AI. It is crucial to develop AI systems that are transparent, fair, and accountable. Organizations must prioritize ethical practices and adopt mechanisms for continuous evaluation and improvement.

AI Implementation:

Implementing AI in organizations requires careful planning and execution. It is crucial to identify the business problem that AI can address, gather relevant data, and select appropriate AI algorithms. Developing a robust infrastructure to support AI implementation, ensuring data privacy and security, and training employees to work with AI systems are key steps in successful AI adoption.

AI Governance:

Governance frameworks play a vital role in shaping the responsible and ethical use of AI. Governments and organizations must establish guidelines and regulations to address concerns related to data privacy, bias, and accountability. Collaborative efforts between policymakers, industry experts, and AI developers are necessary to establish a standardized framework that balances innovation and safeguards societal interests.

Understanding the AI Ecosystem

The AI ecosystem is a complex web of technologies, methodologies, and applications that encompass machine learning, deep learning, natural language processing, and more. To navigate this landscape, one must first grasp the fundamental components:

Machine Learning (ML): This subfield of AI focuses on enabling computers to learn from data and make predictions or decisions. It relies on algorithms and statistical models, often used for tasks like image recognition and predictive analytics.

Deep Learning: A subset of ML, deep learning uses artificial neural networks to process and analyze vast datasets. It has revolutionized tasks such as speech recognition and image classification, and it underpins many cutting-edge AI applications.

Natural Language Processing (NLP): NLP involves the interaction between computers and human language. It is essential for chatbots, sentiment analysis, language translation, and text summarization.

Computer Vision: This field involves enabling computers to interpret and understand visual information from the world, making it vital for applications like facial recognition and autonomous vehicles.

Robotics: AI-driven robotics focuses on creating autonomous systems capable of performing physical tasks. This is vital in manufacturing, healthcare, and even space exploration.

The Role of Data

Data is the lifeblood of AI. Without quality data, AI models are ineffective. When navigating the AI landscape, consider these data-related aspects:

Data Collection: Gathering, preprocessing, and curating data is crucial. Understand the sources and ethical implications of data collection.

Data Quality: Clean, accurate, and representative data is essential. Address issues like bias and data privacy to ensure robust AI solutions.

Data Storage and Management: Effective storage and retrieval of data are key. Cloud solutions, databases, and data warehouses play vital roles in this aspect.

Data Labeling: For supervised learning tasks, data labeling is fundamental. Consider the human resources, tools, and processes required for this task.

The Algorithmic Landscape

Navigating the AI landscape also involves understanding the algorithms at play:

Supervised Learning: In this approach, models learn from labeled data to make predictions. It's widely used for classification and regression tasks.

Unsupervised Learning: Unsupervised learning involves finding patterns in data without labeled examples. Clustering and dimensionality reduction are common applications.

Reinforcement Learning: This approach is used for training agents to make sequences of decisions. It's crucial in areas like robotics and game playing.

Transfer Learning: Transfer learning leverages pre-trained models, adapting them for new tasks. It speeds up model development and is a major trend in AI.

Ensemble Methods: Ensemble methods combine multiple models to improve predictive accuracy and robustness. Bagging and boosting are popular techniques.

Ethical and Regulatory Considerations

Navigating the AI landscape necessitates a strong grasp of the ethical and regulatory framework:

Bias and Fairness: AI systems can inherit biases from data. It's essential to address fairness, transparency, and accountability.

Data Privacy: GDPR, CCPA, and other regulations impact AI projects. Complying with data privacy laws is crucial.

Intellectual Property: Understand patent and copyright implications when using AI technologies. Legal counsel may be required to navigate this complex landscape.

Ethical AI Development: The responsible development and deployment of AI systems is critical. Create guidelines and policies to ensure ethical AI practices.

AI Governance: Develop AI governance structures within your organization to oversee AI projects, manage risks, and ensure compliance with regulations.

Industry Applications

Diverse industries are adopting AI, and understanding their applications can inform your navigation of the AI landscape:

Healthcare: AI is transforming patient care through diagnosis, drug discovery, and personalized treatment plans.

Finance: AI is used for fraud detection, algorithmic trading, and risk assessment.

Retail: Personalized recommendations, inventory management, and chatbots enhance the retail experience.

Manufacturing: AI-driven automation improves production efficiency and quality control.

Transportation: Autonomous vehicles and predictive maintenance are reshaping transportation systems.

Emerging Trends and Challenges

To stay on the cutting edge, it's crucial to keep an eye on emerging trends and challenges in AI:

Explainable AI: Developing models that provide interpretable results is gaining importance, especially in applications like healthcare and finance.

Quantum Computing: Quantum computing has the potential to revolutionize AI by solving complex problems faster.

Edge AI: Processing AI algorithms on edge devices, such as IoT devices or smartphones, is becoming more prominent, enabling real-time decision-making.

AI Ethics and Bias Mitigation: As AI adoption grows, addressing bias and ethical concerns remains a top priority.

AI Talent Shortage: The demand for AI talent is outstripping supply. Organizations need to invest in upskilling and reskilling their workforce.

Building Your AI Strategy

Finally, to effectively navigate the AI landscape, you need a well-defined strategy:

Define Goals: Clearly articulate the problems you want AI to solve and the value it should bring to your organization.

Skill Development: Invest in building AI expertise within your team, either through hiring or training.

Data Strategy: Develop a robust data strategy that covers data collection, quality, and privacy.

Model Selection: Choose appropriate algorithms and models for your specific use case.

Monitoring and Maintenance: Establish processes for monitoring model performance and ensuring timely updates.

Security and Compliance: Implement security measures and compliance checks to protect AI systems and data.

Collaboration: Collaborate with experts, researchers, and organizations in the AI field to stay informed and innovate.

Navigating the AI landscape requires a comprehensive understanding of the technology, data, ethics, regulations, and industry-specific applications. To harness the potential of AI and remain competitive, organizations must continually adapt and refine their strategies in this dynamic and ever-evolving field.

Andrew Mark

CHAPTER THREE

ETHICAL AND LEGAL CONSIDERATIONS IN AI BUSINESS

In the landscape of artificial intelligence (AI) business, success is contingent upon not only technological prowess but also a thorough understanding of ethical and legal principles. This chapter delves into the critical considerations that AI businesses must address, from data privacy and bias mitigation to intellectual property security and compliance with emerging regulations.

1. Data Privacy and Security

Data is the lifeblood of AI, but its usage raises substantial concerns surrounding privacy and security. AI businesses must stick to strict data protection standards to earn the trust of users and regulatory bodies.

2. User Data Privacy

AI companies often collect vast amounts of user data to train their models. Ensuring user consent, transparent data handling practices, and data anonymization are crucial. The EU's General Data Protection Regulation (GDPR) sets a global standard for protecting user data. Compliance with GDPR and other related data privacy regulations is necessary.

3. Data Security

Intrusion and data breaches can have severe effects. AI companies must create robust data security measures, including encryption, access controls, and regular audits, to safeguard sensitive information. Compliance with industry-specific security standards like ISO 27001 is recommended.

4. Bias Mitigation

AI algorithms are subject to bias, which can result in discriminatory outcomes. Mitigating bias is a pressing ethical issue for AI businesses.

5. Training Data Bias

Identifying and rectifying bias in training data is important. Implementing diverse and representative datasets, and continuous monitoring for bias during model development, can help minimize these problems.

6. Explainability and Fairness

AI models must be interpretable and fair. Utilizing explainable AI techniques and fairness algorithms ensures that decision-making processes are clear and non-discriminatory.

7. Ongoing Monitoring

AI businesses should create protocols for ongoing bias monitoring and correction, as AI systems can evolve over time and introduce new biases.

8. Intellectual Property and Patents

Protecting intellectual property is important in the competitive AI industry. Securing patents can protect an AI business's innovations.

9. Intellectual Property Rights

AI companies must create and enforce policies for protecting their intellectual property, including software code, algorithms, and proprietary datasets. Non-disclosure agreements and confidentiality terms can help protect trade secrets.

10. Patent Strategies

Obtaining patents for novel AI algorithms can provide a competitive edge. Engaging with patent attorneys to navigate the complex process of patenting AI inventions is recommended.

11. Open Source Considerations

AI businesses should carefully consider the effects of open-source contributions. While open-source can support innovation, it may also expose proprietary technology to public use. A balance between open-source contributions and proprietary protection is important.

12. Compliance with Emerging Regulations

AI businesses work within a rapidly evolving regulatory environment. To stay ahead, they must constantly adapt to changing laws and regulations.

13. Regulatory Landscape

The regulatory environment for AI is still evolving. AI companies should closely watch developments in their operating regions and aggressively engage with regulatory bodies to help shape emerging regulations.

14. Ethical AI Principles

Adhering to ethical AI principles, such as the IEEE Global Initiative on Ethics of Autonomous and Intelligent Systems, can serve as a guideline even in the absence of specific laws.

15. Risk Assessment and Audits

Conducting regular risk assessments and third-party audits can help ensure compliance with current and future regulations. This may include algorithmic impact assessments, data protection impact assessments, and security checks.

16. Transparency and Accountability

AI businesses should value transparency and accountability in their operations.

17. Model Documentation

Maintaining comprehensive model documentation is important. This should include details on training data, algorithm design, and decision-making methods.

18. User-Facing Transparency

Providing users with clear information about how their data is used and the role of AI in decision-making promotes trust. Transparency reports and easily understandable explanations can enhance user trust.

14. Internal Accountability

Establishing internal accountability structures guarantees that ethical and legal factors are integrated into the company's culture. This may involve specialized ethics committees or officers.

Ethical and legal factors in AI business are inextricably linked to long-term success and societal acceptance. Addressing data privacy, bias mitigation, intellectual property protection, compliance with regulations, and supporting transparency and accountability are essential. AI businesses that prioritize these factors will not only navigate the complex landscape of AI ethics and law but also add to the responsible advancement of this transformative technology.

Part II: Transforming Traditional Industries

CHAPTER FOUR

AI IN AGRICULTURE: GROWING BEYOND LIMITS

The utilization of Artificial Intelligence (AI) in agriculture represents a transformative leap towards sustainable and efficient food production. In this chapter we delve into the practical applications, benefits, and challenges of AI in agriculture, emphasizing its potential to propel the industry beyond its current limits.

PRACTICAL APPLICATIONS OF AI IN AGRICULTURE

Precision Agriculture

Precision agriculture involves the precise management of agricultural inputs to optimize yields while minimizing resource use. AI plays a pivotal role by analyzing data from various sources, such as satellites, drones, and sensors, to provide producers with real-time insights. These insights can inform decisions on irrigation, fertilization, and pest management, ultimately increasing productivity and sustainability.

Crop Monitoring and Disease Detection

AI-powered image recognition and machine learning algorithms can help identify diseases, parasites, and nutrient deficiencies in crops. Using drones or smartphones, farmers can capture images of their fields, and AI can promptly analyze them to detect early signs of problems. By doing so, farmers can take timely actions to mitigate potential injury and reduce crop loss.

Predictive Analytics

AI can process historical and real-time data to predict numerous agricultural outcomes, from weather patterns to market demand. This foresight enables producers to make informed decisions regarding planting, harvesting, and storage, minimizing losses and optimizing profitability.

Crop Yield Estimation

Estimating crop yields accurately is essential for planning and resource allocation. AI models can consider multiple factors, including weather conditions, soil quality, and crop types, to determine yields more precisely. This knowledge enables farmers to adjust their strategies accordingly.

Autonomous Machinery

AI-driven autonomous machinery, such as self-driving tractors and harvesters, can execute tasks more efficiently and accurately than human labor. These devices are equipped with sensors and AI algorithms, allowing them to navigate fields, plant seeds, and harvest crops with minimal supervision. This technology reduces labor costs and increases productivity.

Livestock Management

AI is not limited to agriculture; it also enhances livestock management. Sensors, wearables, and data analytics help monitor animal health, reproduction cycles, and dietary patterns. This data empowers farmers to enhance the well-being of their livestock and optimize production processes.

BENEFITS OF AI IN AGRICULTURE

Increased Productivity

One of the most significant advantages of AI in agriculture is the substantial increase in productivity. By optimizing resource allocation and decision-making, AI helps farmers achieve higher crop yields and better manage their livestock, resulting in more efficient food production.

Resource Efficiency

AI enables the precise utilization of resources such as water, fertilizers, and pesticides. By only applying these inputs when and where they are required, farmers can reduce waste, minimize environmental impact, and cut operational costs.

Improved Sustainability

Sustainable agriculture is a global priority, and AI contributes significantly to this objective. By enhancing resource efficiency, AI helps reduce the environmental footprint of farming, conserving natural resources and fostering ecological balance.

Enhanced Risk Management

AI's predictive analytics provide producers with tools to better manage risks associated with weather fluctuations, market volatility, and crop diseases. With this foresight, they can make informed decisions to mitigate prospective losses.

Labor Savings

Automation and autonomous machinery propelled by AI reduce the need for manual labor in agriculture. This not only reduces labor costs but also addresses labor shortages, making agriculture more attractive and sustainable in regions where the workforce is scarce.

CHALLENGES AND CONSIDERATIONS

Data Privacy and Security

AI in agriculture relies largely on data collection and sharing. Protecting the privacy of this data and securing it against cyber threats is a paramount concern. It is crucial for stakeholders to establish robust data protection mechanisms and encryption protocols.

Adoption Barriers

Adopting AI technology can be costly, and not all producers have the resources or knowledge to implement it. Governments and organizations need to provide incentives and training to help bridge this technology gap.

Ethical Concerns

As AI systems become more integral to agriculture, ethical issues arise, such as the treatment of animals, potential displacement of human labor, and equitable access to AI resources. These concerns must be addressed to ensure responsible and equitable adoption.

Infrastructure and Connectivity

Rural areas often lack the necessary infrastructure and connectivity for AI implementation. Governments and private entities should invest in expanding internet access and developing agricultural technology centers in these regions.

The Takeaway

AI in agriculture is poised to revolutionize the industry, offering solutions to some of its most pressing challenges. By augmenting precision, productivity, and sustainability, AI can enable agriculture to grow beyond its current limitations. However, to completely realize these benefits, stakeholders must address challenges related to data privacy, adoption, ethics, and infrastructure. As AI continues to advance, it will play an increasingly vital role in assuring a more sustainable and productive global food supply.

Andrew Mark

CHAPTER FIVE

REVOLUTIONIZING HEALTHCARE WITH AI

The healthcare industry is on the cusp of a transformation with the incorporation of Artificial Intelligence (AI) technologies. This chapter explores the substantial impact of AI in revolutionizing healthcare, providing detailed examples, and supporting data to elucidate its practical applications. As the demand for high-quality healthcare continues to surge, AI offers innovative solutions to enhance patient care, streamline administrative processes, and improve overall efficiency.

ENHANCING DIAGNOSTICS AND DISEASE PREDICTION

Medical Imaging: AI's applicability in medical imaging has been a game-changer. Deep learning algorithms have demonstrated remarkable accuracy in interpreting medical images such as X-rays, MRIs, and CT scans. For instance, a study conducted by Stanford University (2019) reported that AI algorithms obtained a diagnostic accuracy of 94.6% in detecting pneumonia from chest X-rays, surpassing human radiologists.

Early Detection of Diseases

AI-driven predictive analytics can analyze patient data and detect potential health issues early. IBM Watson's "Watson for Oncology" system, for instance, assists oncologists in creating personalized treatment recommendations. A study published in JAMA Oncology (2018) indicated that Watson's recommendations concurred with human oncologists in breast cancer treatments in 96% of instances.

STREAMLINING ADMINISTRATIVE PROCESSES

Healthcare Chatbots

AI-powered chatbots are increasingly used for scheduling appointments, answering common patient queries, and conducting administrative tasks. According to Accenture, healthcare chatbots can save approximately 20% of physicians' time by automating administrative processes. For example, the Cleveland Clinic implemented a chatbot that scheduled more than 60,000 appointments in its first year, reducing wait times and enhancing patient satisfaction.

Revenue Cycle Management

AI can optimize revenue cycle management by increasing billing accuracy and reducing claim denials. An analysis by Healthcare IT Today revealed that AI-based systems could increase revenue capture by up to 6%. For example, Change Healthcare's AI-enabled system helped Geisinger Health System reduce denials by 65% and increased cash collections by 25%.

PERSONALIZED TREATMENT PLANS

Genomic Medicine

AI enables the analysis of enormous genomic datasets to develop personalized treatment plans. In a landmark study, the Garvan Institute used AI to analyze genetic data from thousands of patients, identifying new genetic markers for various diseases, including cancer and diabetes. This information can guide the development of targeted therapies.

Drug Discovery

Pharmaceutical companies are leveraging AI to accelerate drug discovery. Atomwise, an AI-driven drug discovery company, identified a potential treatment for Ebola in just two days, a procedure that typically takes years. This exemplifies how AI can revolutionize drug development, potentially leading to quicker and more effective treatments for various diseases.

TELEMEDICINE AND REMOTE PATIENT MONITORING

Remote Consultations

AI-powered telemedicine platforms have gained popularity, particularly during the COVID-19 pandemic. For example, Teladoc Health reported a 50% increase in virtual visits in 2020. These platforms offer patients access to healthcare professionals without geographical constraints, enhancing healthcare accessibility.

Remote Patient Monitoring

AI-driven devices can continuously monitor patient vital signs and provide real-time alerts. For instance, the BioSticker, an AI-powered wearable, can monitor physiological data and detect health deteriorations early. Studies have shown a 45% reduction in hospitalizations among patients using such remote monitoring systems.

REDUCING MEDICAL ERRORS AND ENHANCING SAFETY

Medication Safety

AI can substantially reduce medication errors through its ability to cross-reference patient data, drug interactions, and allergies. A study published in the Journal of Medical Internet Research (2020) found that AI-driven medication safety alerts reduced errors by 60% in one healthcare facility.

Predictive Analytics for Patient Safety

AI can predict adverse events and patient deterioration, enabling for proactive interventions. The UPMC (University of Pittsburgh Medical Center) implemented AI models to predict sepsis and obtained a 50% reduction in sepsis-related deaths.

IMPROVING POPULATION HEALTH

Public Health Surveillance

AI is critical in monitoring and responding to public health crises. During the COVID-19 pandemic, AI was used to monitor the spread of the virus, predict outbreaks, and optimize resource allocation. The World Health

Organization (WHO) reported that AI-driven models played a crucial role in mitigating the pandemic.

Epidemiological Studies

AI can analyze large datasets to identify disease trends and risk factors. The HealthMap project, which uses AI to monitor disease outbreaks worldwide, detected the 2014 Ebola outbreak nine days before the World Health Organization's official announcement.

The Takeaway

The integration of AI in healthcare is revolutionizing the industry on multiple fronts. AI is augmenting diagnostics, streamlining administrative processes, enabling personalized treatment plans, facilitating telemedicine and remote patient monitoring, reducing medical errors, and improving population health. The examples and data presented in this chapter underscore the transformative potential of AI in healthcare. As the technology continues to advance, it is imperative for healthcare institutions to embrace AI to provide better care, reduce costs, and ultimately enhance patient outcomes. The future of healthcare is being shaped by AI, and its impact is only anticipated to grow in the years to come.

Andrew Mark

CHAPTER SIX

AI-POWERED RETAIL: FROM BRICK-AND-MORTAR TO CLICK-AND-COLLECT

In this chapter, we look into the transformational impact of artificial intelligence (AI) in the retail business, with a special focus on the move from traditional brick-and-mortar storefronts to the nouvelle click-and-collect model. We will investigate the practical applications of AI in this developing landscape, presenting specific examples and pertinent statistics to highlight the dramatic changes AI has brought to the retail sector.

AI in Retail: An Overview

The retail industry has seen a tremendous metamorphosis in recent years, spurred by the integration of AI technologies. The days of brick-and-mortar stores being the main shopping avenue are long gone, and this development is predominantly owing to AI's diverse skills. AI helps retailers to make data-driven choices, tailor customer experiences, manage supply chains, and enhance overall operational efficiency. Consequently, merchants are switching to a more flexible and responsive approach, illustrated by the click-and-collect concept.

THE CLICK-AND-COLLECT REVOLUTION

Definition and Scope

Click-and-collect, also referred to as "buy online, pick up in-store" (BOPIS), has arisen as a popular buying strategy that combines the convenience of e-commerce with the immediacy of physical retail. Shoppers submit orders online and subsequently collect their items at a selected physical store. AI plays a vital role in enabling the flawless execution of this paradigm.

Practical Implementation

AI-powered click-and-collect systems harness data from many sources to predict consumer demand, optimize inventory levels, and assure effective order fulfillment. For example, Walmart, one of the largest retailers in the world, has incorporated AI-driven systems to predict which products will be in demand, allowing for more precise inventory management. This decreases the likelihood of stockouts and promotes a smoother click-and-collect experience for customers.

Statistics: The Impact of Click-and-Collect

- According to Statista, in 2020, click-and-collect sales in the United States alone amounted to around $58.5

billion, and this figure is anticipated to climb to $83.47 billion by 2022.

- A McKinsey analysis shows that consumers using click-and-collect services climbed by 15-20% during the COVID-19 pandemic.

These data indicate the growing prevalence of click-and-collect in the retail scene.

PERSONALIZATION THROUGH AI

Customer Profiling

One of the primary advantages of AI in the click-and-collect approach is the capacity to develop complete consumer profiles. AI systems evaluate historical purchase data, internet behavior, and demographic information to identify individual preferences. As a result, businesses can give targeted product recommendations, discounts, and promotions, boosting the shopping experience.

Practical Implementation

Amazon is a prime example of a store employing AI for customisation. Their recommendation engine, driven by AI, proposes products to customers based on their browsing and purchase histories. This level of customisation promotes consumer happiness and drives sales.

Statistics: The Impact of Personalization

- A survey by Segment indicated that 71% of consumers feel annoyed when their purchasing experience is impersonal, underlining the significance of customization.
- According to McKinsey, customisation can lead to a sales uplift of 10-30% in the retail sector.

These numbers demonstrate the enormous benefits of AI-driven personalization in the click-and-collect strategy.

INVENTORY MANAGEMENT AND FULFILLMENT

Inventory Optimization

AI-driven algorithms can predict demand trends, helping businesses stock the appropriate products in the correct quantities. This prevents overstocking and decreases waste, resulting in cost savings and enhanced sustainability.

Practical Implementation

Zara, a popular apparel company, leverages AI to optimize inventory and decrease overstock. Their excellent inventory management system ensures that clients can find the things they desire while using the click-and-collect service.

Statistics: The Impact of Inventory Optimization

- Gartner expects that by 2023, AI will enable a 15% improvement in demand forecasting accuracy.

- In 2020, The Home Depot employed AI to optimize their inventory, leading to a 15% drop in out-of-stock items and a 45% reduction in overstock.

These figures demonstrate the usefulness of AI in inventory management and fulfillment.

OPERATIONAL EFFICIENCY AND COST SAVINGS

Supply Chain Optimization

AI-driven algorithms can boost supply chain efficiency by optimizing routes, decreasing transportation costs, and streamlining logistics. This leads in speedier delivery and decreased operational costs.

Practical Implementation

UPS, a global leader in logistics, leverages AI to improve delivery routes, decreasing fuel usage and emissions. This not only boosts their environmental sustainability but also leads to cost savings that can be passed on to consumers.

STATISTICS: THE IMPACT OF OPERATIONAL EFFICIENCY

- DHL's deployment of AI in their supply chain operations resulted to a 10% reduction in operational expenses and a 95% improvement in on-time delivery performance.
- A poll by MHI indicated that 51% of organizations believe that AI and machine learning will greatly improve their supply chain operations.

These numbers indicate how AI may greatly boost operational efficiency and provide cost savings in the retail sector.

The Takeaway

The transformation from traditional brick-and-mortar retail to the click-and-collect model powered by AI is not only a shift in purchasing patterns; it signifies a fundamental change in the way merchants function. The practical uses of AI in customization, inventory management, and supply chain optimization have not only improved customer experiences but have also led cost savings and operational efficiency. As the numbers presented in this chapter illustrate, AI is a vital force in the retail sector, defining the industry's future and assuring its continuous growth and importance in the digital age.

Andrew Mark

CHAPTER SEVEN

AI IN REAL ESTATE: THE SMART PROPERTY SHIFT

Artificial Intelligence (AI) has altered several sectors by improving processes, enhancing decision-making, and giving important insights. The real estate sector is no exception to this revolutionary wave. In this chapter, we look into the applications, benefits, and real-world examples of AI in real estate. By harnessing the potential of AI, the sector is undergoing a paradigm change towards "smart properties," with consequences for buyers, sellers, and agents.

AI-Powered Property Valuation

Property appraisal is a vital phase in real estate transactions. AI has changed this procedure, making it more accurate and efficient. Using enormous databases, AI algorithms can assess historical property sales, market patterns, and even environmental elements to produce correct property appraisals.

Example: Zillow's Zestimate uses AI to estimate property values with amazing accuracy. It examines data points such as location, square footage, and recent transactions to generate immediate values for millions of homes.

Stat: Zillow's Zestimate claims a median error rate of just 1.9% nationally, illustrating the precision AI can attain in home valuation.

Predictive Analytics for Investment

Investors and property developers can benefit from AI-driven predictive analytics. Machine learning models examine market patterns, historical data, and economic indicators to uncover profitable investment possibilities. These models help stakeholders make educated decisions and maximize their portfolios.

Example: Redfin's Investment Score employs AI to analyze potential investment properties. It evaluates elements including price patterns, local amenities, and future developments to anticipate property appreciation.

Stat: Redfin reports a 95% accuracy rate in predicting property appreciation, highlighting the significance of AI in investment decisions.

Enhanced Customer Experience

AI technology have transformed client experiences in real estate. Chatbots and virtual assistants offer 24/7 service, answering questions, scheduling property viewings, and providing information about properties.

This promotes client satisfaction and streamlines the buying process.

Example: Compass, a real estate company, uses AI-powered chatbots to assist clients. These chatbots connect with users, ask pertinent questions, and deliver individualized property recommendations.

Stat: According to a research by Inside Real Estate, 84% of real estate agents reported higher customer satisfaction when employing AI-powered chatbots.

Smart Marketing and Targeted Advertising

AI enables real estate professionals to design highly focused marketing efforts. Algorithms evaluate user activity, tastes, and demographics to adapt adverts, ensuring that listings reach the proper audience and optimize exposure.

Example: Facebook Ads employs AI to provide tailored real estate adverts to users who have recently looked for homes or expressed interest in real estate-related content.

Stat: AI-driven advertising on Facebook has shown a 30% boost in conversion rates compared to non-targeted advertising efforts.

Property Management and Maintenance

AI plays a crucial role in property management and upkeep. Smart sensors and IoT devices can monitor property conditions, detect faults, and even schedule maintenance automatically. This minimizes operations costs and increases the overall property experience.

Example: Smart apartment complexes like The Kelvin in Houston employ AI to manage lighting, heating, and cooling depending on resident preferences and occupancy, resulting in a 15% savings in energy expenses.

Stat: According to a survey by the National Apartment Association, 72% of property managers reported a decrease in maintenance expenses and a 24% reduction in tenant complaints after deploying AI-driven property management systems.

Risk Assessment and Fraud Prevention

AI assists in identifying risks linked with real estate transactions and avoids fraudulent activity. Machine learning algorithms can identify possible red flags, such as anomalies in property paperwork, to safeguard buyers and sellers from scams.

Example: Fannie Mae utilizes AI algorithms to spot anomalies in mortgage applications, minimizing the risk of fraudulent loans and defaults.

Stat: Fannie Mae claimed a 45% decrease in mortgage fraud cases since using AI-based risk assessment tools.

The Takeaway

AI's influence in the real estate market is definitely disruptive. It's opening the road for "smart properties" that offer better appraisal accuracy, improved investment prospects, richer customer experiences, and more effective property management. As the real estate business continues to embrace AI, stakeholders will profit from the efficiency, accuracy, and insights it brings. The numbers and examples provided in this chapter highlight the actual benefits AI brings in changing the future of real estate.

Andrew Mark

CHAPTER EIGHT

AI-DRIVEN FINANCE: FROM BANKING TO WEALTH MANAGEMENT

In recent years, Artificial Intelligence (AI) has transformed the finance business, revolutionizing the way traditional banking services are given and enhancing wealth management tactics. This chapter analyzes the critical role AI plays in transforming the financial landscape, giving real examples and pertinent facts to highlight its impact.

The Evolution of AI in Finance

The application of AI technologies in finance has been an evolutionary process, highlighted by the growing integration of AI-powered tools and systems across multiple financial sectors. Banks and financial institutions have implemented AI to streamline their operations, improve customer service, and gain a competitive edge. Wealth management organizations have used AI to better investing strategies and give personalized services to clients.

AI IN BANKING

Customer Service and Chatbots

AI-driven chatbots have become crucial tools in the banking business. These chatbots address normal client queries, give account information, and even aid in executing transactions. They give consumers speedy and effective service, available 24/7. According to a survey by Juniper Research, chatbots are estimated to save banks around $7.3 billion by 2023.

Example: Bank of America's virtual assistant, Erica, has successfully handled millions of client requests and helped customers save time by giving pertinent financial information.

Fraud Detection

AI is a great partner in the fight against financial fraud. Machine learning algorithms examine transaction data to discover unusual patterns and highlight possibly fraudulent behavior. In 2020, Javelin Strategy & Research observed that banks implementing AI-based fraud detection systems witnessed a 15% reduction in losses related to fraud.

Example: Citibank utilizes machine learning to identify anomalous spending trends, helping prevent illegal transactions.

Credit Scoring

Traditional credit scoring techniques are often limited in measuring a borrower's risk. AI-driven credit scoring algorithms can consider a wider range of data, such as social media activity and online conduct, delivering a more accurate estimate of an individual's creditworthiness.

Example: ZestFinance employs machine learning to provide alternative credit ratings, extending credit to individuals who may be missed by traditional models.

AI IN WEALTH MANAGEMENT

Robo-Advisors

Robo-advisors have rocked the wealth management sector by delivering automated investing advice based on individual goals and risk tolerance. As of 2020, the Aite

Group predicted that assets managed by robo-advisors exceeded $1.4 trillion globally.

Example: Wealthfront, a major robo-advisor, manages over $25 billion in assets and creates diversified portfolios for its clients.

Portfolio Optimization

AI-driven portfolio optimization algorithms regularly monitor market data and adapt investment portfolios to optimize returns while avoiding risk. This dynamic approach to wealth management has achieved outstanding outcomes. According to a study by BlackRock, AI-managed portfolios beat human-managed portfolios by 35% over a five-year period.

Example: Hedge firms like Bridgewater Associates use AI algorithms to optimize their portfolios, resulting in huge gains for their customers.

Sentiment Analysis

AI tools are applied to analyze market sentiment by scanning news articles, social media messages, and financial information. This study helps wealth managers make informed investment decisions and respond to quickly changing market conditions.

Example: Kensho, a financial data analytics startup, employs natural language processing and machine learning to evaluate market news and deliver insights to traders and investors.

AI's Impact on Customer Experience

The integration of AI technologies has dramatically improved client experience across banking and wealth management. Customers now benefit from more personalized services, quicker response times, and access to advanced financial analytics.

In a survey performed by Deloitte in 2021, 80% of financial institutions said that AI had improved the client experience, resulting in higher customer happiness and loyalty.

Challenges and Ethical Considerations

Despite the huge benefits of AI in finance, there remain obstacles and ethical considerations to solve. One important concern is the possibility for prejudice in AI algorithms, which may lead to biased lending practices or investing judgments. To tackle this, regulators and industry stakeholders are drafting rules and standards for ethical AI use in banking.

The Takeaway

AI has not only changed the finance industry but also brought up new potential for banks and wealth management organizations to expand their offerings and streamline operations. From improved customer service and fraud detection to sophisticated investing strategies, the influence of AI is clear. As AI continues to improve, its role in banking is likely to expand even further, benefiting both institutions and clients alike.

In a world where data and technology are important, financial institutions that embrace AI-driven solutions will remain at the forefront of the industry, delivering greater services and achieving huge cost savings. The future of finance is clearly entwined with artificial intelligence, making it vital for financial professionals to stay informed and adapt to this fast expanding field.

Part III: Emerging AI Frontiers

CHAPTER NINE

SMART CITIES: AI-POWERED URBAN INNOVATION

In recent years, the term "Smart Cities" has become a buzzword, grabbing the imagination of urban planners, policy officials, and technology enthusiasts throughout the world. These cities are envisioned as lively hubs of innovation, sustainability, and efficiency, where technology plays a major role in addressing urban difficulties. One of the main aspects driving the transition of smart cities is Artificial Intelligence (AI). We will explore the ways AI-powered urban innovation is reshaping the current urban scene, using real-world examples and statistics that underline the significance of this disruptive technology.

AI-Enhanced Traffic Management

Traffic congestion is a prevalent issue in cities across the globe. AI delivers novel solutions for efficient traffic management and increasing the overall quality of urban living. Cities like Singapore have developed AI-powered traffic management systems that leverage real-time data from sensors, cameras, and GPS devices to monitor and control traffic flow. As a result, traffic congestion in Singapore has reduced by 25%, resulting in a considerable decrease in carbon emissions and travel times.

Predictive Policing and Public Safety

AI has changed law enforcement and public safety in smart cities. Predictive policing models employ historical crime data to discover patterns and spend resources wisely. The Los Angeles Police Department (LAPD) reported a 33% drop in property crimes after installing an AI-driven predictive policing system, indicating the potential for AI to increase public safety.

Sustainable Resource Management

Sustainability is a basic principle of smart cities. AI aids in sustainable resource management by optimizing energy use, waste management, and resource allocation. For instance, Copenhagen, Denmark, employs AI to improve waste collection routes, resulting in a 30% reduction in fuel use and a drop in CO_2 emissions.

Healthcare and Telemedicine

The healthcare sector in smart cities is undergoing substantial revolution through AI. Telemedicine and AI-powered diagnostic technologies have become crucial in providing efficient and accessible healthcare services. In Barcelona, Spain, an AI-driven telemedicine technology cut emergency hospital visits by 30%, saving both time and resources.

Public Transportation Optimization

AI-driven public transportation systems promote mobility, reduce traffic congestion, and improve the overall quality of life. London's Transport for London (TfL) employs AI algorithms to enhance bus schedules and routes. This project resulted to a 13% increase in ridership and an 18% reduction in accidents, illustrating the practical benefits of AI-powered public transportation.

Smart Grids and Energy Efficiency

Energy usage in smart cities is being optimized by AI-powered smart grids. By evaluating real-time data, AI systems can efficiently distribute electricity and prevent energy loss. Amsterdam's smart grid initiative resulted in a 20% reduction in energy consumption and a large drop in greenhouse gas emissions.

AI-Powered Waste Management

Efficient waste management is vital for the cleanliness and sustainability of smart cities. AI helps cities like Tokyo, Japan, streamline garbage collection by anticipating when and where bins need emptying. This predictive method lowered collection expenses by 30% and greatly decreased the amount of overflowing trash bins.

Infrastructure Maintenance

Maintaining urban infrastructure is a hard and costly endeavor. AI-powered predictive maintenance solutions help smart cities save money and time. For example, New York City employs AI to monitor the structural condition of bridges and tunnels, saving maintenance expenditures by 15% and assuring safer transit for citizens.

Enhanced Emergency Response

AI allows speedier and more effective emergency response in smart cities. In the instance of wildfires in San Diego, California, AI-powered algorithms assessed real-time weather and topographical data to anticipate fire trajectories. This allowed authorities to respond rapidly and evacuate communities, lessening the impact of the wildfires on lives and property.

Public Engagement and Smart Governance

AI-driven chatbots and virtual assistants have proved crucial in boosting public participation and facilitating efficient government in smart cities. Singapore's Virtual Singapore initiative, for example, uses AI chatbots to give information and services to citizens. This project resulted in a 15% increase in citizen involvement with government services.

The Takeaway

AI-powered urban innovation is a vital ingredient in determining the future of smart cities. As evidenced by the countless real-world examples and statistics, AI boosts traffic management, improves public safety, optimizes resource management, transforms healthcare, and revolutionizes several other elements of urban living. Smart cities that incorporate AI technology are not only more efficient and sustainable but also provide a superior quality of life for its citizens. The future of urbanization clearly belongs to AI-powered smart cities, and as technology continues to improve, the opportunities for innovation are unlimited.

CHAPTER TEN

AI IN EDUCATION: SHAPING THE FUTURE OF LEARNING

In the previous chapters, we addressed the essential ideas and historical context of AI. Here we go deeper into the practical aspects of using AI in education, highlighting its revolutionary potential and offering real-world examples and statistics to explain the influence it has on the future of learning. We will investigate the ways in which AI is transforming various elements of education, from individualized learning to administrative efficiency.

Personalized Learning

Personalized learning has emerged as one of the most significant benefits of incorporating AI into education. AI-powered solutions have the flexibility to adapt to the particular demands and learning styles of each student.

According to a survey by EdTech Magazine, schools that have embraced individualized learning through AI have witnessed a 20-60% rise in student competency ratings.

Example 1: Adaptive Learning Platforms

Adaptive learning platforms, such as Knewton and DreamBox, leverage AI algorithms to assess a student's strengths and weaknesses. These platforms then generate custom-tailored learning routes and exercises to satisfy those unique demands. Research undertaken by the Bill and Melinda Gates Foundation demonstrated that children using such platforms exhibited a 25-30% gain in test performance compared to traditional classroom techniques.

Example 2: Chatbots for Student Support

AI-powered chatbots are being employed to deliver real-time support to pupils. Georgia State University claimed a 50% boost in student retention rates after introducing an AI chatbot named "Pounce." The chatbot offered students individualized instruction and answered their queries, ensuring they had the support they needed when they needed it.

ADMINISTRATIVE EFFICIENCY

AI has also shown to be a game-changer in enhancing the administrative efficiency of educational institutions. The adoption of AI in administrative tasks not only reduces the workload but also minimizes human error.

Example 3: Student Enrollment and Registration

The University of Texas at Austin adopted an AI-driven enrolling system that decreased enrollment processing time by 90%. This system uses natural language processing to analyze and approve enrollment paperwork, allowing personnel to focus on other value-added duties.

Example 4: Predictive Analytics for Resource Allocation

Many colleges now employ predictive analytics powered by AI to allocate resources more efficiently. For instance, the University of Washington witnessed a 30% reduction in energy expenses by utilizing AI to predict building usage patterns and optimize heating and cooling systems.

CONTINUOUS ASSESSMENT AND FEEDBACK

AI's capacity to deliver immediate feedback and assessment is altering the way kids learn and teachers instruct.

Example 5: Automated Grading Systems

AI-driven grading systems, like Gradescope and Turnitin, are becoming common in educational institutions. These systems provide immediate and consistent feedback to students, considerably lowering grading time for professors. In a research conducted at Stanford University, AI-based grading indicated a 35% reduction in grading time for instructors.

Example 6: Early Intervention Systems

AI can examine student performance data to identify those who may be failing academically. Arizona State

University reported that its early intervention approach, which employed AI, increased retention rates by 7%. This technology enables the university to deliver timely support to students who needed it most.

FUTURE POSSIBILITIES

As AI continues to evolve, the opportunities for its incorporation into education are unlimited. Here are some trends and future prospects for AI in education:

Example 7: Virtual Reality (VR) and Augmented Reality (AR) in Education

AI-driven VR and AR experiences can boost student engagement and deliver immersive learning environments. According to a report by Gartner, by 2025, 60% of colleges would employ VR and AR for educational purposes.

Example 8: AI Tutors and Mentors

AI tutors like ScribeSense and mentorship platforms like MentorMob are set to deliver individualized, on-demand learning aid to pupils. These platforms leverage AI to deliver explanations and instruction in a conversational and interactive manner.

The Takeaway

AI in education is undoubtedly impacting the future of learning, with its potential to tailor lessons, streamline administrative duties, provide constant feedback, and offer intriguing future possibilities. The facts and examples given in this chapter demonstrate the concrete influence of AI in educational contexts. As we move forward, it is vital for educational institutions to embrace this transformative technology to guarantee that students receive the greatest possible education and are equipped for the challenges of the 21st century. The future of learning is now, and AI is at the vanguard of this educational revolution.

CHAPTER ELEVEN

AI IN ENTERTAINMENT: CRAFTING PERSONALIZED EXPERIENCES

In the domain of entertainment, AI has opened up intriguing prospects to design tailored experiences for audiences. This chapter digs into the convergence of AI and entertainment, highlighting how AI is altering the business by increasing content development, curation, and audience interaction.

CONTENT CREATION

AI-Generated Music and Art

AI algorithms have proven essential in making music and art that resonate with individual inclinations. One outstanding example is OpenAI's DALL-E, a model capable of creating visuals from verbal descriptions. It can produce personalized images for books or make unique artwork for album covers. Additionally, AI-generated music platforms like Amper Music and AIVA can develop tailored soundtracks for many reasons, including video games and marketing.

Scriptwriting and Storytelling

AI has been utilized in scriptwriting and storytelling to examine data, trends, and audience preferences. For instance, ScriptBook, an AI-driven script analysis tool, rates scripts based on their prospective economic success. Moreover, ChatGPT, a conversational AI, may assist screenwriters and authors by providing creative prompts, character development ideas, and storyline suggestions.

Content Generation for Video Games

In the gaming business, AI has been applied to create procedural content, enriching the player's experience with dynamic and ever-changing game worlds. No Man's Sky, a popular game, leverages AI algorithms to construct enormous, diverse planets for players to explore. This enables an infinite gameplay experience by building distinct landscapes and ecosystems with each session.

CONTENT CURATION

Personalized Streaming Recommendations

Streaming companies like Netflix, Amazon Prime, and Spotify have leveraged the power of AI to propose content tailored to individual preferences. By studying user activity, AI systems offer movie and music suggestions that fit with a viewer's or listener's tastes. This strategy dramatically enhances the user experience and fosters longer interaction.

Curating News and Articles

AI-driven news aggregators, such as Flipboard and Google News, build personalized news feeds by considering a user's reading history and interests. This guarantees that visitors receive relevant and entertaining material while keeping them informed about topics they care about.

AUDIENCE ENGAGEMENT

Chatbots and Virtual Assistants

AI-powered chatbots and virtual assistants are being increasingly used in entertainment to communicate with viewers. For instance, during live events or broadcasts, chatbots can answer queries, provide real-time updates, and offer interactive experiences. The employment of chatbots in sporting events, concerts, and online gaming has witnessed a boom in popularity.

Virtual Reality (VR) and Augmented Reality (AR)

AI has played a significant role in developing VR and AR experiences. Companies like Oculus and Magic Leap employ AI to enhance immersion in virtual environments by mimicking realistic interactions, spatial audio, and individualized avatars. This breakthrough has transformed gaming, training, and even remote social interactions, making them more personalized and engaging.

CASE STUDIES AND STATISTICS

Netflix's Recommendation System

Netflix's recommendation system, powered by AI, is a prime illustration of content curation's success. It's believed that over 80% of the content watched on Netflix is discovered through recommendations, highlighting the influence of AI in keeping viewers engaged with personalized content.

AI-Generated Music's Popularity

In 2022, AI-generated music started gaining acceptance in the mainstream music industry. "SounBeamer," an AI-generated song by OpenAI, was listened over 2 million times on Spotify within its first week of release, illustrating the public's growing interest in AI-generated music.

AI in Video Game Development

Games like "No Man's Sky" and "Minecraft" have achieved enormous popularity thanks to AI-driven procedural content generation. "No Man's Sky" has an active player community of over 15 million players as of

2022, illustrating the attraction of AI-enhanced gaming experiences.

Personalized Marketing in Entertainment

AI-driven tailored marketing initiatives have resulted in a considerable boost in audience engagement. For instance, Spotify claimed a 26% increase in user engagement and a 31% rise in premium subscriptions after deploying AI-driven tailored playlists in 2020.

The Takeaway

AI is transforming the entertainment industry by delivering the tools and skills to design individualized experiences for audiences. Whether through content creation, curation, or audience involvement, AI is transforming the way we consume and interact with entertainment. With the continuous progress of AI technology, we may expect a future where entertainment experiences become even more personalized to individual interests, boosting our enjoyment of movies, music, games, and more.

CHAPTER TWELVE

AI AND SUSTAINABILITY: GREENING THE BUSINESS WORLD

In the age of environmental consciousness and corporate responsibility, corporations are under increasing pressure to embrace sustainable practices. The integration of Artificial Intelligence (AI) into different parts of corporate operations offers a valuable tool for addressing sustainability concerns. This chapter covers the dramatic impact of AI on sustainability in the corporate sector, presenting practical insights, real-world examples, and statistics to highlight how AI is revolutionizing and greening the business landscape.

AI'S ROLE IN SUSTAINABILITY

1. Resource Optimization

AI plays a crucial role in optimizing resource utilization, a critical part of sustainability. AI-driven algorithms are capable of evaluating massive datasets to detect inefficiencies and offer improvements. For instance, predictive maintenance powered by AI can reduce machinery downtime, saving energy and lowering the need for raw materials.

Example: General Electric has employed AI to boost the efficiency of its wind turbines. By forecasting maintenance needs, they have decreased downtime by up to 20%, resulting to significant energy savings.

2. Supply Chain Efficiency

Sustainable supply chain management is crucial for minimizing carbon footprints. AI can boost visibility and control in supply chains by forecasting demand, optimizing routes, and minimizing waste in logistics.

Example: Walmart has leveraged AI to optimize its supply chain, leading to a 10-15% decrease in transportation costs and a considerable reduction in greenhouse gas emissions.

3. Renewable Energy

AI can contribute in the development and administration of renewable energy sources such as solar and wind. Machine learning algorithms can forecast energy generation and consumption trends, assuring efficient energy production.

Example: Google's DeepMind employed AI to control energy use in its data centers, resulting in a 15% reduction in overall energy usage.

AI FOR SUSTAINABLE AGRICULTURE

Sustainable agriculture is vital for feeding the world's rising population while conserving resources. AI technology have the potential to change farming techniques.

1. Precision Agriculture

AI-driven precision agriculture involves using sensors, drones, and machine learning to optimize farming operations. This strategy minimizes the usage of water, pesticides, and fertilizers.

Example: John Deere's AI-powered tractors analyze soil data to plant crops more efficiently, resulting in lower resource usage and increased yields.

2. Crop Monitoring

AI can scan satellite photos and provide insights on crop health and yield predictions. This aids in efficient pest control and irrigation.

Example: Microsoft's FarmBeats employs AI to evaluate data from numerous sources to assist farmers make data-driven decisions. It has resulted in a 30% reduction in water usage.

AI IN WASTE MANAGEMENT

Efficient waste management is a vital part of sustainability. AI can assist in garbage sorting, recycling, and minimizing waste generation.

1. Smart Waste Bins

AI-powered sensors can recognize and sort waste, making recycling more effective.

Example: The city of Barcelona, Spain, installed AI-driven smart bins, which decreased waste collection expenses by 30% and boosted recycling rates by 50%.

2. Waste Prediction

Machine learning algorithms can forecast garbage generation patterns, helping municipalities optimize waste pickup schedules.

Example: The city of San Francisco used AI to improve their rubbish collection routes, resulting in a 40% reduction in fuel use.

AI AND SUSTAINABLE FINANCE

The world of finance is not spared from the pressure for sustainability. AI can assess ESG (Environmental, Social, and Governance) data to help sustainable investing decisions.

Statistics: According to a survey by PwC, 77% of institutional investors believe AI can assist identify ESG risks and opportunities.

Example: BlackRock, one of the world's largest asset managers, leverages AI to examine ESG issues in investment choices, with $2.5 trillion in assets under management focused on sustainable investing.

THE FUTURE OF AI AND SUSTAINABILITY

As the usage of AI in business continues to grow, its impact on sustainability is likely to increase. By 2030, AI is predicted to contribute up to $15.7 trillion to the global economy, with major contributions to sustainability efforts.

Statistics: A research by McKinsey believes that AI can help cut global greenhouse gas emissions by 16%, which is comparable to eliminating the total present emissions of the European Union.

The Takeaway

AI is a great tool for addressing sustainability concerns in the corporate world. From resource optimization to sustainable agriculture, waste management, and sustainable finance, AI-driven solutions are altering the way businesses function. Real-life examples and statistics demonstrate the real benefits of incorporating AI into sustainability efforts, indicating that AI is definitely greening the business sector. As corporations continue to embrace AI for sustainability, we can look forward to a more ecologically responsible and economically viable future.

Part IV: Entrepreneurship in AI

CHAPTER THIRTEEN

STARTING YOUR AI BUSINESS: FROM IDEA TO IMPLEMENTATION

The realm of artificial intelligence is evolving rapidly, and it gives endless chances for entrepreneurs to utilize this technology. However, the path to developing a successful AI firm is plagued with hurdles and complexities. We will examine the important processes, methods, and real-world examples to guide you through this revolutionary process.

Section 1: Defining Your AI Business Idea

Identifying Market Needs

Before jumping into the AI business sector, it is necessary to discover a true market demand. Look for areas where AI can solve problems more efficiently or provide new opportunities.

Example: Grammarly, an AI-powered writing aid, addresses the need for improved writing and communication skills.

Validating Your Idea

Conduct rigorous market research to validate your AI company idea. Analyze competition, demand, and potential barriers to entry.

Example: Freenome, a firm leveraging AI for early cancer detection, did significant clinical trials to validate their hypothesis.

Section 2: Assembling Your Team

Expertise in AI

Building a great AI team is crucial. You need data scientists, machine learning engineers, and domain specialists to collaborate cohesively.

Example: OpenAI's diversified workforce includes leading AI researchers, engineers, and domain specialists, allowing breakthroughs like GPT-3.

Diversity and Collaboration

Diversity in your team's background and experiences can bring fresh ideas and innovative solutions.

Example: Diversity at NVIDIA, a top AI hardware and software business, adds to their success in numerous AI sectors.

Section 3: Developing a Prototype

Proof of Concept

Develop a prototype or proof of concept to illustrate your AI idea's practicality and potential utility.

Example: DeepMind's AlphaGo, a prototype AI system, revealed AI's potential to outperform human champions in complex games.

Iterative Development

Use an iterative strategy to enhance your AI model. Collect comments and continue improve.

Example: IBM's Watson evolved through iterations to become a robust AI platform for numerous applications.

Section 4: Data Acquisition and Management

Data Sourcing

Access to reliable data is pivotal for AI development. Secure relevant and clean data sources.

Example: Tesla's autonomous driving AI relies on a massive collection of real-world driving experiences.

Data Privacy and Ethics

Adhere to stringent data privacy and ethical standards. Ensure compliance with rules such as GDPR and CCPA.

Example: Facebook's AI Research division focuses on creating AI while preserving user privacy.

Section 5: Model Development and Training

Model Selection

Choose the proper AI model for your business. It can be a neural network, reinforcement learning, or natural language processing model, depending on your needs.

Example: OpenAI's GPT-3, a versatile language model, has been deployed in different sectors from content generation to customer service chatbots.

Training and Validation

Train your AI model on your data, then thoroughly validate its performance. Utilize techniques like cross-validation and hyperparameter tweaking.

Example: Google's BERT model, used for natural language processing, underwent significant training and validation methods.

Section 6: Scaling and Implementation

Infrastructure

Invest in the necessary infrastructure to deploy your AI solution at scale. Cloud services like AWS, Azure, and Google Cloud can be invaluable.

Example: Netflix leverages AI algorithms to personalize content suggestions on a global scale utilizing AWS infrastructure.

Integration and Deployment

Integrate your AI solution easily into the target environment. This may entail building APIs or proprietary software interfaces.

Example: Amazon's recommendation engine, powered by AI, is incorporated into their e-commerce platform, delivering individualized product choices.

Section 7: Performance Monitoring and Optimization

Real-time Monitoring

Continuously monitor the performance of your AI system in real-time. Set up notifications for anomalies and difficulties.

Example: Twitter employs AI to identify and filter out harmful content, with real-time monitoring for effective moderation.

Continuous Learning

Implement reinforcement learning and update your AI model depending on new data and user feedback.

Example: Spotify's music recommendation engine grows over time by learning from users' listening patterns.

Section 8: Regulations and Compliance

Legal Compliance

Comply with legal norms and standards connected to AI, assuring responsible and ethical use.

Example: The European Union's AI Act sets up restrictions for AI applications to ensure transparency and safety.

Ethical Considerations

Be cognizant of ethical considerations in AI, such as fairness, bias, and transparency.

Example: Microsoft's responsible AI principles stress justice and transparency in AI development.

The Takeaway

Starting an AI firm involves a multidimensional path, from ideation to full-scale implementation. The journey is tough, but the opportunities are infinite. By recognizing market needs, assembling a capable team, designing a prototype, handling data properly, training models carefully, and negotiating legal restrictions, you can drive your AI firm towards success. As the AI field continues to grow, it is vital to stay informed with the newest advancements and ethical standards, ensuring that your AI business positively influences society and the future of technology.

With devotion and effort, you can develop your AI company idea into a thriving reality, contributing to the ongoing revolution in the field of artificial intelligence.

CHAPTER FOURTEEN

FUNDING YOUR AI VENTURE: INVESTORS AND OPPORTUNITIES

In the dynamic field of artificial intelligence (AI), getting the necessary capital to power your startup is a vital step towards realizing your entrepreneurial ambition. AI has altered several areas, including healthcare, banking, and education, and the potential for innovation and growth is huge. This chapter covers the numerous funding alternatives available to AI businesses, the sorts of investors interested in AI enterprises, and provides practical insights on navigating the competitive landscape of AI investing.

I. THE AI INVESTMENT LANDSCAPE

The AI investment landscape is a varied ecosystem, offering various paths for securing the financial resources required to nurture and grow your enterprise. These include:

Bootstrapping: Many successful AI firms began with low resources and relied on personal savings or small loans to get off the ground. For example, OpenAI, one of the pioneers in AI research, was first supported by a group of high-profile IT entrepreneurs, including Elon Musk and Sam Altman.

Angel Investors: Angel investors are affluent individuals who invest their personal resources in enterprises in exchange for equity. They are attracted to AI companies due to the prospect of disruptive technology and large returns on investment. A well-known example is Reid Hoffman, co-founder of LinkedIn, who has invested in many AI businesses like Xnor.ai.

Venture Capital: Venture capital firms are essential actors in the AI investment landscape, typically giving large funding in exchange for ownership and playing an active role in the creation and development of businesses. For instance, Data Collective DCVC, a venture capital firm, specializing in AI and deep tech investments and has supported startups like Vicarious and Vicarious Surgical.

Corporate Investors: Many multinational organizations are actively investing in AI startups as part of their innovation and digital transformation agendas. For example, Google's parent firm, Alphabet, has invested in various AI projects, such as DeepMind and Waymo.

Crowd-funding: Crowdfunding platforms like Kickstarter and Indiegogo provide entrepreneurs the possibility to acquire capital from a wide spectrum of individual contributors. AI-related campaigns, such as Jibo, have effectively exploited crowdsourcing to jumpstart their ventures.

II. TYPES OF INVESTORS

Understanding the sorts of investors and their investment techniques is vital for adapting your pitch and gaining the correct funding for your AI venture.

Seed Investors: Seed investors are often the first to invest in startups, providing the initial funds needed to validate an idea or construct a prototype. They hunt for breakthrough AI solutions and visionary creators. For example, Y Combinator is known for developing early-stage AI businesses, including OpenAI.

Early-Stage Venture Capitalists: Early-stage VCs, such as Sequoia Capital and Andreessen Horowitz, specialize on investing in firms that have already built a product or prototype. They assist startups scale and attain the next level of growth.

Late-Stage Venture Capitalists: Late-stage VCs like SoftBank Vision Fund and General Catalyst invest in more mature AI firms that are poised for expansion. These investors are searching for proven products, market momentum, and a viable business model.

Strategic Investors: Strategic investors are frequently corporations with a specific interest in your sector or technology. They can provide not only financial support but also key relationships and distribution channels.

NVIDIA, for example, invests in AI firms that may exploit their GPU technology.

III. SECURING FUNDING FOR YOUR AI VENTURE

To attract investors and win funding for your AI venture, it's vital to offer a compelling argument. Here are some practical steps:

Develop a Strong Value Proposition: Clearly describe the problem your AI solution solves and the unique value it brings. Provide real-world examples of how your technology can make a difference. For instance, Udacity, an AI-powered online education platform, efficiently fulfills the requirement for scalable, individualized learning experiences.

Build a Skilled Team: Investors place a high premium on a capable and experienced team. Highlight the qualifications and competence of your team members, notably in AI and related topics. Grammarly, an AI-powered writing assistance, features a staff with strong AI and language processing expertise.

Show Traction and indicators: Prove that your product is gaining traction in the market by showing user adoption, revenue growth, and important performance indicators. For instance, Suki.AI, an AI-powered medical assistant, has shown significant success in lowering administrative tasks for healthcare practitioners.

Intellectual Property: If your AI venture is built on unique technology or algorithms, protect your intellectual property. Investors will be more interested if they realize that your innovations are defensible. DeepMind, famed for its innovative AI research, has a robust portfolio of patents.

Create a Roadmap: Outline your ambitions for the future, including product development, market expansion, and revenue growth. Investors want to know how their investment will be used to move the endeavor ahead.

The Takeaway

Securing finance for your AI company is a tough yet critical step in defining the future of AI innovation. The scene is packed with opportunities, from individual angel investors to corporate giants, all wanting to help the next big breakthrough. By understanding the many funding possibilities, types of investors, and writing a compelling pitch, you can boost your chances of fulfilling your AI vision and contributing to the ever-evolving world of artificial intelligence. Remember, it's not only about getting financial resources; it's about finding the proper partners that share your vision for the future of AI.

CHAPTER FIFTEEN

AI BUSINESS STRATEGIES: MARKETING, SCALING, AND MONETIZATION

Leveraging AI for business strategy is no longer an option; it's a must. Let's consider the important parts of AI business strategies, focusing on marketing, scalability, and monetization, to shed light on how organizations can harness the power of AI to thrive in today's competitive climate.

AI IN MARKETING: A PARADIGM SHIFT

The importance of AI in marketing is evident, with organizations increasingly relying on AI-driven solutions to achieve a competitive edge. AI helps marketers to better understand consumer behavior, boost personalization, and make data-driven decisions.

Personalized Recommendations

AI-driven recommendation systems, like the ones used by Netflix and Amazon, have grown pervasive. These systems evaluate client data to deliver targeted product or content recommendations. According to a research by McKinsey & Company, individualized recommendations can lead to a 30% increase in income.

Example: Netflix's recommendation system evaluates viewing habits, preferences, and user behavior to suggest content, enhancing consumer engagement and retention.

Predictive Analytics

Predictive analytics powered by AI is transforming marketing by projecting future trends and customer behavior. It helps organizations manage resources more efficiently and plan marketing efforts with higher accuracy.

Example: E-commerce behemoth, Alibaba, employs predictive analytics to forecast consumer demand, leading to a 10% increase in sales.

Chatbots and Customer Service

Chatbots and virtual assistants empowered with AI are revolutionizing customer service. They offer 24/7 help, handle questions swiftly, and boost client happiness. Statista says that the worldwide chatbot market is anticipated to reach $1.25 billion by 2025.

Example: H&M's chatbot provides clients with fashion advise, cutting response time and increasing customer experience.

SCALING USING AI

Scaling a firm has always been a struggle, but AI presents new options for growth. Companies can extend operations, optimize processes, and access new markets by employing AI-driven scaling solutions.

Automation

Automation is a vital part of scaling. AI-powered robotic process automation (RPA) can handle monotonous jobs, freeing up human resources for more value-added operations. The market for RPA is estimated to reach $2.9 billion by 2027, according to Grand View Research.

Example: UiPath, a leading RPA supplier, enabled a financial services organization reduce processing time by 75%, enabling them to manage more clients.

Supply Chain Optimization

AI is revolutionizing supply chain management by boosting visibility, forecasting demand, and optimizing logistics. According to a survey by MarketsandMarkets, the AI in supply chain market is predicted to increase from $1.1 billion in 2021 to $7.1 billion by 2026.

Example: Walmart leverages AI to optimize its supply chain, lowering out-of-stock items by 30% and improving overall efficiency.

Market Expansion

AI can assist firms in discovering unexplored markets and designing methods to enter them. Analyzing market data and consumer behavior patterns, AI can help organizations increase their reach.

Example: Airbnb uses AI to study travel trends and provide hosts with insights into demand, encouraging expansion into new regions.

MONETIZING AI: THE PATH TO PROFIT

Monetizing AI investments is vital for enterprises. While AI can increase productivity and consumer satisfaction, it also offers various options for direct money generating.

Subscription Models

Many AI-driven goods and services operate on subscription models. Companies charge users a regular fee to access AI-powered features or content.

Example: Adobe's Creative Cloud delivers AI-enhanced functionality in its design tools, attracting millions of customers and creating a consistent stream of cash.

Data Monetization

Data is a precious asset, and AI can help extract actionable insights from it. Companies can monetize data by selling it to third parties or using it to generate new products and services.

Example: Waze, a navigation app, monetizes its real-time traffic data by selling it to municipal planners and advertisers.

AI as a Service

AIaaS (AI as a Service) is an emerging market. Companies offer AI capabilities as a service, allowing others to integrate AI into their applications without large initial expenses.

Example: Google Cloud's AI Platform delivers a wide range of AI services, enabling organizations to harness AI without substantial expenditures in infrastructure.

The Takeaway

AI has radically revolutionized the way businesses work, from marketing strategies to scaling and monetization. Companies that embrace the promise of AI in these areas are more likely to thrive in the competitive business environment. The facts and examples offered in this chapter indicate that AI is not simply a buzzword; it's a practical instrument for changing the future of business.

As businesses continue to implement AI, it is vital to be informed about the newest advances and best practices in AI strategy. In the next chapters, we will discuss AI ethics, regulatory considerations, and the future of AI in the corporate sector, providing a thorough roadmap to navigating the AI landscape.

Part V: Case Studies

CHAPTER SIXTEEN

AI BUSINESS SUCCESS STORIES

Let's begin with these success stories.

GOOGLE'S DEEPMIND

Google's DeepMind, a subsidiary of Alphabet Inc., has made waves in the world of artificial intelligence (AI) with its extraordinary achievements, particularly in healthcare. DeepMind's route to success highlights the revolutionary potential of AI in addressing some of the most complicated and crucial situations in the world.

DeepMind's triumphs may be traced back to its early developments, including the AlphaGo project, which defeated the world champion Go player in 2016. This triumph marked a key milestone in the application of AI to strategic decision-making, setting the groundwork for ever more ambitious endeavors.

However, it was in the healthcare industry that DeepMind truly made its mark. The company's AI algorithms have been applied to alter the way medical practitioners diagnose and treat patients. One of the most prominent breakthroughs occurred in the form of a collaboration with Moorfields Eye Hospital, where DeepMind's AI technology successfully recognized eye illnesses, such as diabetic retinopathy, with a high degree of accuracy. This discovery not only improved patient outcomes but also helped decrease the burden on healthcare staff by automating the screening process.

DeepMind's work with the Royal Free London NHS Foundation Trust resulted in Streams, an app aimed to assist physicians control patient deterioration more efficiently. The software uses AI to warn healthcare providers to possible issues and streamline patient care, leading to speedier responses and better patient outcomes. Another surprising success story for DeepMind is its work with the U.S. Department of Veterans Affairs to forecast patient deterioration. By evaluating huge volumes of health data, DeepMind's AI system may forecast patient deterioration, allowing for early intervention and saving lives in the process.

The success of DeepMind's healthcare projects shows the great potential of AI in enhancing patient care, making healthcare more efficient, and saving lives. Moreover, DeepMind's commitment to resolving concerns about patient data privacy and security has created a great precedent for responsible AI research in healthcare.

Beyond healthcare, DeepMind continues to push the boundaries of AI in different disciplines, from natural language understanding to robotics and quantum computing. Its successes show the vast possibilities that AI offers and serve as an inspiration for other companies attempting to harness AI's potential for both corporate success and societal benefit. DeepMind's journey from a research lab to a transformational force in healthcare and beyond serves as a shining illustration of the capacity of AI to make the world a better place.

IBM WATSON

IBM's Watson has revolutionized various industries. In healthcare, it assists doctors in making more accurate diagnoses. In finance, it helps identify trading patterns and investment opportunities. Watson's natural language processing capabilities have been instrumental in customer support chatbots.

MD Anderson Cancer Center: In the field of healthcare, IBM Watson has partnered with the MD Anderson Cancer Center to revolutionize oncology. By analyzing vast amounts of medical literature and patient data, Watson for Oncology helps doctors make data-driven treatment decisions. This has improved the speed and accuracy of cancer diagnoses, ultimately leading to more successful outcomes for patients.

Royal Bank of Scotland (RBS): RBS has used IBM Watson to enhance customer service through its chatbot, "Luvo." Luvo assists customers with inquiries, simplifying the resolution of common banking issues. This has resulted in faster response times and improved customer satisfaction, while also reducing operational costs.

General Motors: The automotive industry is also benefiting from AI. General Motors uses IBM Watson's AI capabilities to enhance the driving experience through its OnStar Go platform. This platform leverages Watson's natural language processing to provide personalized in-car experiences, such as making restaurant reservations, finding nearby gas stations, and even ordering coffee while on the go.

Woodside Energy: In the energy sector, Woodside Energy, an Australian oil and gas company, utilizes IBM Watson for predictive maintenance. By analyzing data from sensors on their equipment, Watson can predict when maintenance is needed, reducing downtime and saving significant costs.

H&R Block: IBM Watson has transformed the way taxes are prepared. H&R Block uses Watson to assist tax professionals and clients in finding tax deductions they might have otherwise missed. This results in more accurate tax returns and higher customer satisfaction.

These success stories highlight how IBM Watson's AI capabilities have had a positive impact across a range of industries, from healthcare to finance, automotive, energy, and even tax services. These applications of AI have not only improved operational efficiency but also enhanced customer experiences and led to more informed decision-making, ultimately contributing to the success of these businesses.

TESLA'S AUTOPILOT

Tesla's Autopilot is an AI-driven advanced driver-assistance system. It demonstrates the potential of AI in the automotive industry by enabling semi-autonomous driving. It's constantly evolving and enhancing safety on the road.

Tesla's Autopilot system has been at the forefront of the automotive industry's use of artificial intelligence and autonomous driving technology. Since its inception, it has not only caught the interest of the public but also set the benchmark for AI-driven automotive innovation. Here's a basic review of Tesla's Autopilot success story:

Innovation and Early Adoption: Tesla introduced Autopilot in 2015 as an enhanced driver-assistance system, merging hardware and software to enhance vehicle safety and convenience. This marked a huge step toward AI-driven autonomous driving, pioneering technologies like adaptive cruise control, lane-keeping, and self-parking.

Continuous Improvement: Tesla's iterative approach to Autopilot development and deployment has been a crucial success factor. The business regularly upgrades and refines the system through over-the-air software updates. This ensures that Autopilot-equipped vehicles become smarter and safer over time.

Safety Record: While Autopilot's deployment wasn't without controversy and accidents, Tesla's data showed a constantly increasing safety record, with Autopilot-enabled cars being statistically safer than those without the system. This data-driven approach has helped establish trust in the technology.

Autonomous Milestone: In 2020, Tesla stated its ambitious aim to attain full self-driving capability. While this aim hasn't been fully reached, Tesla's continual improvements in AI and autonomous technologies have brought the industry closer to the reality of self-driving cars.

Market Dominance: Tesla's Autopilot performance has had a major impact on the electric vehicle market, putting Tesla as a leader in the sector. The Autopilot technology has been a strong selling point for Tesla automobiles, contributing to the company's large market share and growth.

Regulatory hurdles: Tesla's Autopilot path hasn't been without hurdles. Striking the appropriate balance between innovation and safety has led to scrutiny from regulators, but the company's willingness to engage with authorities and adapt its technology has been vital to its success.

Inspiring Competitors: Tesla's achievements with Autopilot have spurred other automotive and tech companies to invest extensively in AI and autonomous driving. The success of Tesla's Autopilot has ignited an industry-wide rush to create self-driving technologies.

Tesla's Autopilot is a stunning illustration of how AI-driven innovation can transform traditional sectors, challenge limits, and spark a wave of technical improvements. It stands as a light for the future of transportation, where AI is poised to play an increasingly major role.

AMAZON'S RECOMMENDATION ENGINE

Amazon's recommendation system uses AI to analyze customer data and provide personalized product recommendations. This has greatly increased sales and customer satisfaction on their platform.

Amazon's recommendation engine is a superb example of AI-driven business success. It's a cornerstone of their e-commerce business, and its success has led to outstanding outcomes. Here are some crucial elements about this AI success story:

Personalized Shopping Experience: Amazon's recommendation engine leverages AI algorithms that assess a user's prior purchases, browsing history, and behavior on the site to deliver highly personalized product recommendations. This has dramatically boosted user engagement and happiness.

Increased Sales and Revenue: By suggesting products that customers are more likely to buy, Amazon has enjoyed a large rise in sales and revenue. The engine not only improves the sales of popular things but also promotes the discovery of lesser-known products.

Enhanced client Retention: AI recommendations boost client loyalty. Amazon's ability to understand and forecast customer preferences keeps users coming back, lowering churn and improving customer lifetime value.

Operational Efficiency: AI-driven recommendations also optimize inventory management and save costs. Amazon can better estimate demand for specific products, hence eliminating overstock and out-of-stock situations.

Diverse Applications: Amazon's recommendation system isn't restricted to only proposing things. It also powers their video streaming platform (Amazon Prime Video) and Kindle eBook suggestions. This highlights the adaptability of AI in driving corporate success.

Continuous Improvement: Amazon invests extensively in developing its recommendation system. They constantly apply machine learning techniques to make their forecasts more accurate, including real-time data and customer feedback into the algorithms.

Third-party Services: The success of Amazon's recommendation engine has led to it selling comparable services to third-party vendors through Amazon Web Services (AWS). This opens up new revenue sources by sharing AI-driven recommendation technology with other firms.

In essence, Amazon's recommendation engine is a prime example of how AI may change e-commerce and produce tremendous financial success. By generating a more personalized shopping experience, increasing sales and revenue, strengthening customer retention, improving operational efficiency, and expanding its applications, Amazon continues to set the benchmark for AI success in the commercial world.

NETFLIX'S CONTENT RECOMMENDATION

Netflix's AI-driven recommendation system suggests content to users based on their viewing history. This technology has played a pivotal role in keeping subscribers engaged, ultimately driving growth for the company.

Netflix's content recommendation system is a prominent example of AI-driven success in the business world. With millions of subscribers worldwide, Netflix relies on cutting-edge AI algorithms to keep viewers engaged and delighted. Here are several crucial factors that make it a success story:

Personalized Content Recommendations: Netflix leverages machine learning algorithms to examine user data, such as viewing history, preferences, and ratings. This data is utilized to give individualized content recommendations for each viewer, boosting their overall streaming experience.

Retention and Engagement: AI-driven recommendations are vital for client retention and engagement. By proposing material that corresponds with users' interests, Netflix keeps customers hooked, reducing churn rates and boosting the time spent on the network.

Efficient Content Discovery: With a wide collection of titles, finding anything to watch might be overwhelming. Netflix's AI streamlines content discovery, making it easier for consumers to locate movies and shows that fit their taste, hence increasing content consumption.

Cost Savings: By automating content recommendations, Netflix lowers the need for manual curation, which can be costly and time-consuming. AI streamlines the process, allowing Netflix to distribute resources more efficiently.

Content Production: Netflix also employs AI to make data-driven judgments on original content production. By evaluating viewership habits and preferences, the platform may invest in series and movies that are likely to resonate with its audience, contributing to its distinctive content library.

A/B Testing: Netflix regularly fine-tunes its recommendation algorithms using A/B testing, ensuring that the system develops with changing viewer preferences and habits.

Internationalization: Netflix's AI models adapt to varied cultural preferences and languages, allowing it to provide a worldwide audience with bespoke recommendations.

Netflix's AI-driven content recommendation engine is a spectacular success story in the world of business. It not only promotes customer satisfaction but also contributes to the platform's continued expansion and global appeal. Through the strategic use of AI, Netflix has altered the way people discover and consume content, setting a bar for other organizations wanting to harness the power of artificial intelligence.

SALESFORCE'S EINSTEIN

Salesforce's AI platform, Einstein, helps businesses leverage AI for customer relationship management. It aids in predicting customer needs, automating routine tasks, and enhancing the overall customer experience.

Salesforce Einstein has been instrumental in driving AI business success stories across numerous industries. Here are a few famous examples:

Unilever:

Consumer goods giant Unilever utilized Salesforce Einstein to boost its customer relationship management. The organization employed AI-powered data to better understand client preferences and offer personalized marketing communications. This resulted in a huge jump in consumer engagement and a 20% increase in conversion rates.

T-Mobile:

T-Mobile, a renowned telecoms firm, deployed Salesforce Einstein to strengthen its customer service operations. By employing AI for predictive analytics and chatbots, they realized a 40% reduction in customer care response times, leading to enhanced customer happiness and loyalty.

UBS:

UBS, a major financial services corporation, used Salesforce Einstein to improve its wealth management services. The AI-driven insights supplied financial advisors with real-time information on market movements and individualized investment recommendations, resulting in a 25% rise in assets under management.

L'Oreal:

The beauty and cosmetics major L'Oreal incorporated Salesforce Einstein to revolutionize its marketing strategies. By analyzing consumer data, they produced individualized product suggestions and marketing strategies. This technique led to a 15% gain in online sales and better client retention.

American Red Cross:

Non-profit organizations have also profited from Salesforce Einstein. The American Red Cross employed AI to optimize their blood donation programs. By forecasting supply and demand patterns, they decreased blood shortages by 30% and enhanced the efficiency of their operations.

These success stories show the versatility of Salesforce Einstein in helping businesses across multiple sectors to leverage the potential of artificial intelligence, enhance customer experiences, and drive development. Whether it's in marketing, customer service, finance, or non-profit operations, AI-powered solutions have shown to be a game-changer for these businesses.

AIRBNB'S DYNAMIC PRICING

Airbnb uses AI to optimize pricing for hosts based on factors such as demand, location, and property type. This has not only helped hosts maximize their revenue but also increased Airbnb's bookings and revenue.

Airbnb, a global leader in the hospitality sector, has harnessed artificial intelligence (AI) to strengthen its business processes and improve the experience for both hosts and guests. One of the most noteworthy AI-driven innovations at Airbnb is its Dynamic Pricing system.

Dynamic Pricing is an algorithmic pricing methodology that modifies the nightly rates of Airbnb listings in real-time based on numerous criteria such as demand, supply, location, seasonality, and even local events. This sensible pricing technique enables hosts to optimize their earnings by setting competitive prices, while guests may access listings at rates that reflect current market conditions.

Here are a few main reasons why Airbnb's Dynamic Pricing is considered a stunning success story in the AI business world:

Optimizing Revenue: Airbnb hosts sometimes struggle to decide the optimal price for their rentals. With Dynamic Pricing, hosts no longer need to manually alter their charges. The AI technology performs it for them, enhancing their odds of attracting guests while optimizing their earnings.

Improved Guest Experience: By setting competitive prices that match market realities, Airbnb ensures that guests may obtain lodgings at reasonable costs. This helps to guest happiness and encourages repeat bookings.

Scalability: With millions of listings globally, maintaining price manually at such a scale would be an exhausting undertaking. Dynamic Pricing, powered by AI, efficiently scales to include all Airbnb properties, making it a vital tool for the company's continuing expansion.

Data-Driven Insights: Airbnb's AI algorithms evaluate massive amounts of data, giving important insights for both hosts and the firm itself. These information assist hosts understand their property's performance and trends, while Airbnb can make informed decisions to improve its platform.

Competitive Advantage: Airbnb's application of AI-driven Dynamic Pricing provides it a competitive edge in the sharing economy. This technology helps the platform maintain its market leadership by delivering superior pricing strategies and overall user experience.

In essence, Airbnb's Dynamic Pricing is a testament to the good impact of AI in the commercial world. By employing AI to optimize pricing, Airbnb has not only enhanced its host and guest experiences but has also positioned itself as a pioneer in the travel and hospitality sector. This success story illustrates the potential of AI to change established business structures and foster innovation in varied industries.

MICROSOFT'S AZURE AI

Microsoft's AI solutions, integrated into Azure, are used across various industries. From predictive maintenance in manufacturing to personalized marketing in retail, Azure AI has empowered businesses to make data-driven decisions.

Microsoft's Azure AI has been a driving force behind countless success stories across various industries. Here are a few instances of AI business success stories powered by Azure AI:

Jabil: Jabil, a worldwide manufacturing solutions supplier, uses Azure AI to boost its predictive analytics capabilities. By incorporating machine learning and AI models, Jabil improved its supply chain processes. This resulted to reduced downtime, enhanced inventory management, and increased production efficiency, resulting in large cost savings.

Bosch: Bosch, a prominent provider of technology and services, used Azure AI to develop novel solutions for the Internet of Things (IoT). By employing Azure's machine learning capabilities, Bosch produced predictive maintenance and monitoring solutions for industrial equipment. These technologies have helped companies prevent costly breakdowns and enhance operational efficiency.

Schneider Electric: Schneider Electric, a global specialist in energy management and automation, leveraged Azure AI to construct EcoStruxure, a comprehensive IoT and AI platform. EcoStruxure lowers energy usage, decreases operational costs, and enhances sustainability in numerous industries, from buildings to data centers.

Anheuser-Busch InBev: The world's largest brewing firm, Anheuser-Busch InBev, teamed with Microsoft Azure to optimize its brewing processes. By utilizing Azure AI, they deployed machine learning algorithms to increase quality control and predictive maintenance, resulting to greater beer quality and reduced production downtime.

Maersk: Maersk, a worldwide shipping giant, deployed Azure AI to optimize its shipping and logistics operations. By applying machine learning and AI for route optimization, container tracking, and cargo monitoring, Maersk improved delivery accuracy and lowered fuel usage, resulting in considerable cost savings and environmental benefits.

Carnival Corporation: Carnival Corporation, a major cruise line operator, integrated Azure AI into its cruise ships to enhance visitor experiences. They employed AI-driven insights to tailor onboard experiences, improve safety, and optimize ship operations, leading to increased customer happiness and operational efficiency.

Siemens: Siemens, a worldwide technological powerhouse, joined with Azure AI to develop MindSphere, an industrial IoT platform. MindSphere allows firms to connect, monitor, and analyze their industrial equipment in real-time. This has helped organizations enhance equipment performance, reduce downtime, and make data-driven decisions.

These success stories highlight how Microsoft's Azure AI is impacting organizations across industries by enabling them to leverage the power of artificial intelligence and machine learning. Whether it's optimizing industrial processes, improving supply chain logistics, increasing customer experiences, or expanding sustainability efforts, Azure AI continues to play a critical role in driving innovation and success for companies globally.

FACEBOOK'S DEEPTEXT

Facebook employs AI through DeepText, which helps in understanding and categorizing the vast amount of content posted on the platform. This ensures better user engagement and targeted advertising.

Facebook's DeepText is a stunning success story in the domain of artificial intelligence, exhibiting the ability of AI in revolutionizing the world's largest social media network. This breakthrough natural language processing (NLP) system, developed by Facebook in 2016, has played a crucial role in increasing user experiences and helping businesses interact with their target audiences.

DeepText's success depends in its capacity to interpret and evaluate the textual content posted on the site, making it more relevant for users. Here are a few crucial features of this AI company success story:

Improved User Experience: DeepText helps Facebook to give more tailored and relevant content to its users. By recognizing the intricacies of language, sentiment, and context, it can customize a user's feed more effectively, displaying them posts, adverts, and material that are more aligned with their interests.

Enhanced Ad Targeting: Businesses benefit from DeepText's capacity to target their adverts to a more receptive audience. This not only boosts the effectiveness of advertising on the platform but also leads in a greater return on investment.

Multilingual Support: DeepText's multilingual capabilities have been vital in growing Facebook's global reach. It can understand and process content in many languages, making the platform accessible to a bigger and more diversified user base.

Content Moderation: The AI system also plays a vital role in content moderation by recognizing and eliminating improper or dangerous information, delivering a safer and more positive user experience.

Efficient Customer service: Facebook employs DeepText for customer service with automated responses and content analysis. This streamlines the process and addresses user inquiries more efficiently.

The success of DeepText has not only enhanced user engagement but has also produced enormous money for Facebook by offering businesses with a highly effective advertising platform. It highlights the potential of AI to improve user experiences and drive business growth in the digital era, making it a compelling AI business success story in the world of social media.

ALIBABA'S AI IN RETAIL

Alibaba uses AI in its Hema supermarkets, employing technologies like facial recognition for payments and personalized shopping recommendations. This has revolutionized the retail experience in China.

Alibaba, the e-commerce giant from China, has been a forerunner in the integration of artificial intelligence (AI) within the retail sector. Their inventive use of AI technology has not only enhanced the shopping experience for consumers but has also boosted their bottom line. Here's a brief look at Alibaba's AI business success story in retail:

Personalized Shopping Recommendations:

Alibaba's AI systems scan massive quantities of client data to deliver personalized product recommendations. By studying the particular interests, shopping history, and behavior of each consumer, Alibaba may propose products that are more likely to be of interest. This customisation has dramatically enhanced sales and customer happiness.

Smart Inventory Management:

AI-powered algorithms help Alibaba manage its massive inventory efficiently. Predictive analytics and demand forecasting algorithms optimize stock levels and decrease surplus inventory, lowering costs and waste.

Cashier-less Stores:

Alibaba proposed the concept of "Tao Cafe" stores, which combine AI and computer vision to allow customers to shop without traditional cashiers. Shoppers may pick up products and just walk out, with the AI system tracking their decisions and charging their accounts. This innovation streamlines the shopping process, decreases labor expenses, and enhances the shopping experience.

Customer Service Chatbots:

Alibaba deploys AI-driven chatbots to answer customer concerns and support requests. These virtual assistants are available 24/7 and can swiftly resolve consumer concerns, contributing to enhanced customer service and satisfaction.

Visual Search:

Alibaba's AI enables users to search for products using images or descriptions, making the buying experience more straightforward and accessible. This technology recognizes and matches visual patterns, letting consumers discover the objects they want more simply.

Supply Chain Optimization:

AI is utilized to optimize Alibaba's supply chain, from sourcing products to delivering them. This enhances the efficiency and accuracy of order fulfillment, assuring timely deliveries and decreasing operational costs.

Fraud Detection:

Alibaba employs AI to detect fraudulent activities and transactions, safeguarding both customers and sellers on its platform. The technology can identify suspicious behavior and take measures to prevent fraudulent transactions.

Alibaba's success in retail AI is a tribute to the company's devotion to technological innovation. Their use of AI has not only streamlined operations but has also produced a more personalized and convenient shopping experience for customers. As a result, Alibaba has continued to lead the way in the e-commerce market, setting a high benchmark for AI integration in retail.

OPENAI'S GPT-3:

OpenAI's GPT-3, like the AI model you're interacting with, is being used for various applications, from content generation and chatbots to language translation. Its potential for natural language understanding is opening up new opportunities in content creation and customer service.

OpenAI's GPT-3 has been a game-changer for enterprises across numerous industries, allowing new solutions and producing spectacular success stories. Here are a few AI business success stories powered by GPT-3:

Copywriting and Content Generation: Many companies have included GPT-3 into their content marketing strategies. It can write high-quality blog posts, product descriptions, and even ad text. By automating content generation, businesses have saved time and resources while preserving consistency and quality.

Virtual Assistants and client Support: GPT-3 has been used to construct AI-powered virtual assistants and chatbots that can answer client requests efficiently. They can provide rapid responses and aid with various jobs, freeing up human agents for more difficult issues. This has resulted to greater customer satisfaction and cost savings for enterprises.

Language Translation: GPT-3's multilingual capabilities have enabled businesses to deliver real-time translation services for their clients. Whether it's in-app chat translation or website content translation, this has opened up new markets and enhanced global accessibility for products and services.

Medical Diagnostics: GPT-3's natural language processing skills have been employed in the medical profession. It can help doctors and medical practitioners with detecting problems, recommending treatment alternatives, and even deciphering dense medical literature, thereby enhancing patient care and outcomes.

Content Recommendations: Many content platforms, such news websites and streaming services, have exploited GPT-3's ability to give highly tailored content recommendations. This not only promotes user engagement but also increases the time users spend on their platforms, leading into more ad income and subscription prices.

Market Analysis and Predictions: GPT-3 can evaluate enormous volumes of data and assist in making data-driven decisions. It has been applied in financial institutions for market analysis, risk assessment, and even predicting trends, offering organizations a competitive edge in the fast-paced financial world.

Product Development: Businesses are using GPT-3 to develop ideas for new products or services. By studying client input and market trends, it can recommend novel ideas, perhaps leading to the development of successful, customer-centric goods.

E-commerce Personalization: GPT-3 has proved crucial in upgrading the e-commerce experience. It may evaluate user behavior and preferences to deliver highly personalized product recommendations and even generate product descriptions targeted to specific shoppers, enhancing conversion rates and income.

Education and Training: GPT-3 has been applied in the construction of tailored e-learning platforms. It can build customized lesson plans, answer student queries, and even offer interactive content, making online education more engaging and successful.

These success stories highlight how GPT-3's adaptability and language understanding have altered numerous elements of business operations. As AI technology continues to improve, it's probable that additional success stories will surface, further highlighting the worth and promise of AI in the commercial world.

NVIDIA'S GPUS:

Nvidia's GPU technology has been a crucial enabler of AI development. It's used in a wide range of applications, from autonomous vehicles to medical imaging, and has played a vital role in advancing AI capabilities.

NVIDIA's GPUs have been essential in producing AI business success stories across multiple industries. Here are a few famous examples:

Healthcare Diagnostics: Companies like PathAI and Butterfly Network have exploited NVIDIA GPUs to produce improved medical imaging solutions. These technologies enable clinicians make more precise diagnoses and improve patient outcomes by processing medical pictures, such as MRIs and CT scans, with amazing precision.

Autonomous Vehicles: The autonomous car industry has made considerable advancements, mainly to NVIDIA's GPUs. Companies like Waymo and Tesla employ NVIDIA's technology for its self-driving cars. These GPUs enable real-time processing of huge volumes of data from sensors, allowing vehicles to travel safely and effectively.

Financial Services: In the finance sector, AI-powered algorithms are utilized for fraud detection, algorithmic trading, and risk assessment. Companies like Capital One and Citadel Securities have used the power of NVIDIA GPUs to process enormous volumes of financial data, leading to more efficient and secure financial services.

Retail and E-commerce: Retailers like Amazon have enhanced their supply chain management and consumer experience with AI. They leverage NVIDIA GPUs to power recommendation algorithms, inventory management, and cashier-less businesses. This has resulted in higher customer satisfaction and increased operational efficiency.

Manufacturing and Industry 4.0: Manufacturing companies, such as Siemens and Foxconn, have integrated AI into their production processes. NVIDIA GPUs assist in quality control, predictive maintenance, and robotics control. This has resulted to higher production and reduced downtime.

Energy & Environmental Conservation: Companies like DeepMind have leveraged NVIDIA GPUs for AI-driven solutions to minimize energy use in data centers, decreasing environmental impact. These technologies not only enhance the bottom line but also contribute to sustainability goals.

Entertainment & Gaming: NVIDIA's gaming GPUs, notably the GeForce series, have not only altered gaming experiences but also driven AI in the entertainment business. Video game makers, such as Epic Games and Ubisoft, employ these GPUs for realistic graphics, physics simulations, and AI-driven game mechanisms.

NVIDIA's GPUs have become a driving factor behind many AI success stories by providing the processing capacity necessary for training and deploying AI models. Their adaptability and performance have made them a cornerstone in different industries, contributing to tremendous developments and economic progress.

These AI success stories illustrate the transformative power of artificial intelligence across diverse industries, revolutionizing the way businesses operate and engage with their customers. As AI continues to advance, we can expect even more remarkable success stories to emerge in the future.

CHAPTER SEVENTEEN

AI BUSINESS FAILURES: LESSONS TO LEARN FROM

Artificial Intelligence (AI) has surely altered several areas, delivering novel solutions and potential developments. However, it is crucial to understand that not all AI efforts have been successful. This chapter dives into several noteworthy AI business failures, highlighting the insights they offer to entrepreneurs, investors, and industry professionals.

CASE STUDY 1: JUICERO

In 2016, Juicero, a start-up with an ambitious vision, planned to improve the way people drink fresh juice by building a premium juice-making machine. The device was connected to the internet and required proprietary juice packs, which users would feed into the machine. These packs were designed to be fresher and more handy than regular juice.

Lesson 1: Over-engineering and Overpricing

Juicero's demise illustrates the need of combining innovation with cost-effectiveness. The equipment was overly complex and expensive, priced at $399. The company's customized juice packs also imposed major recurring costs. Consequently, consumers found it more inexpensive and feasible to prepare juice using traditional methods.

Lesson 2: Fostering Genuine Utility

Juicero's failure serves as a warning that AI-driven goods should adapt to real user demands. Entrepreneurs must ask whether their products actually improve people' lives and whether these advantages justify the price tag.

CASE STUDY 2: CHATGONE

ChatGone, a firm that debuted in 2017, sought to employ AI to change the customer support sector. Their computerized chatbots promised personalized, quick customer care. Despite initial enthusiasm, the company saw a quick fall.

Lesson 3: Ethics and Transparency

ChatGone's concerns revolved around the opacity of their AI-driven chatbots. Customers became more uncomfortable with the chatbots' capacity to impersonate people successfully. This led to concerns about data privacy and dishonesty, hurting the company's brand.

Lesson 4: Long-term Viability

ChatGone tells us that the quest of instant success can lead to shortcuts that threaten long-term viability. Startups must examine the ethical consequences of their AI solutions, especially in areas where openness and trust are key.

CASE STUDY 3: BLOCKBLUNDERS

BlockBlunders, created in 2018, aims to harness AI to forecast cryptocurrency movements. Their algorithms promised to enhance profits in the risky bitcoin industry.

Lesson 5: The Hype Trap

BlockBlunders' failure serves as a cautionary tale on the over-hyping of AI capabilities. Promising assured success in bitcoin trading was unsustainable and misleading, resulting to large customer losses.

Lesson 6: Robust Data and Testing

For AI enterprises in fields like bitcoin, rich data and comprehensive testing are important. BlockBlunders ignored the relevance of past market data and rigorous testing of their AI models, leading to incorrect predictions.

CASE STUDY 4: ZOOMCAR

ZOOMCar, an automobile rental service established in 2020, incorporates AI for vehicle maintenance scheduling and maximizing fleet usage. They wanted to cut operational costs while boosting consumer experiences.

Lesson 7: Scalability and Integration

ZOOMCar's failure underlines the significance of scalable integration of AI technology. The corporation struggled to integrate AI across their huge fleet. Their inability to incorporate the technology smoothly led to increasing maintenance expenses and service disruptions.

Lesson 8: Employee Training and Adaptation

The case of ZOOMCar underlines the significance of comprehensive employee training when using AI. A lack of understanding and preparedness among staff can prevent the seamless integration of AI technologies.

THE BROADER PERSPECTIVE

In addition to these case studies, there are several broad lessons that may be gleaned from these AI business failures:

Lesson 9: Realistic Expectations

Entrepreneurs and investors should keep realistic expectations regarding AI. AI is a tremendous tool, but it is not a panacea. Success may not be instant, and dangers should be acknowledged.

Lesson 10: Customer-Centric Approach

Customers' requirements and input should be at the forefront of AI business development. Understanding the target audience and consistently responding to their tastes and concerns is vital.

Lesson 11: Responsible AI

Responsible AI standards, including transparency, ethics, and data privacy, are non-negotiable. Neglecting these standards can lead to public outrage and regulatory problems.

Lesson 12: Flexibility and Adaptation

The business landscape is continuously developing. AI organizations must be nimble, able to react to changing market situations, technical breakthroughs, and client preferences.

The Takeaway

The AI business landscape is replete with both achievements and disasters. These case studies provide significant insights into the problems that AI startups can confront. By learning from these failures and using the lessons mentioned in this chapter, entrepreneurs, investors, and industry professionals may make better informed decisions and establish more resilient and profitable AI-driven enterprises. It is via these mistakes that we may pave the route for a more sustainable and responsible AI future.

SEIZING THE AI GOLD MINES

AI has proven to be a game-changer in the business world, giving rise to what can be aptly described as "AI Gold Mines." These gold mines represent untapped reservoirs of potential, waiting to be harnessed for businesses seeking a competitive edge.

AI in Finance: A Treasure Trove of Insights

The financial sector is one of the first to recognize the potential of AI. Banks and financial institutions are using AI to enhance customer experiences, streamline operations, and manage risk. For instance, JPMorgan Chase employs machine learning algorithms to predict loan defaults with 90% accuracy, thus minimizing potential losses. According to a study by PwC, 72% of financial service companies have adopted AI, leading to a potential cost reduction of 22% by 2030.

Healthcare: Revolutionizing Patient Care

AI has become a valuable asset in the healthcare industry. It is being used to improve diagnostics, patient care, and drug discovery. IBM's Watson, for example, analyzes patient records and medical literature to suggest personalized treatment plans. The global AI in healthcare market is expected to reach $31.3 billion by 2025, with a CAGR of 41.4%. This represents a significant opportunity for companies to tap into the AI gold mine within the healthcare sector.

Retail: Transforming Customer Engagement

Retailers are leveraging AI to transform customer engagement, optimize inventory management, and enhance the overall shopping experience. Amazon's recommendation system, driven by AI algorithms, is a prime example. According to a report by Retail Perceptions, 61% of shoppers prefer stores that offer personalized experiences. This signifies the potential for businesses to tap into the AI gold mine by enhancing customer engagement.

Manufacturing: Maximizing Efficiency

Manufacturers are deploying AI to optimize production processes, improve quality control, and predict equipment maintenance. Siemens, for instance, uses AI to analyze sensor data and predict equipment failures, reducing downtime and maintenance costs. According to a report by Accenture, AI in manufacturing can increase productivity by up to 40%, highlighting the gold mine of efficiency improvements AI offers.

Agriculture: Precision Farming

AI is transforming agriculture through precision farming, where data-driven decisions enhance crop yields and reduce resource wastage. John Deere's See & Spray technology uses computer vision and machine learning to precisely target herbicide application, reducing usage by 77%. With the global population expected to reach 9.7 billion by 2050, the agricultural AI market is poised to grow, providing fertile ground for companies to seize opportunities.

Energy: Enhancing Sustainability

AI is aiding the energy sector in optimizing power generation, reducing emissions, and enhancing grid management. Google's DeepMind has demonstrated a 40% reduction in energy consumption for data centers using AI. As the world shifts towards sustainability, companies that harness the AI gold mine in the energy sector can lead the way in environmental stewardship.

Education: Personalized Learning

The education sector is not exempt from AI's transformative power. AI-driven platforms can tailor education to individual learning styles, improving retention rates and knowledge acquisition. Pearson's AI-driven tutor, for instance, adapts lessons to each student's progress. As education technology continues to evolve, the AI gold mine within the education sector becomes more apparent, with the global AI in education market expected to reach $20.84 billion by 2027.

SEIZING THE AI GOLD MINES

To seize the opportunities presented by AI, organizations need a strategic approach:

a. **Identify Business Needs:** Begin by identifying specific areas where AI can bring value. Consider customer engagement, operational efficiency, data analysis, and decision-making processes.

b. **Data Collection and Management:** AI relies on high-quality data. Establish robust data collection and management processes to ensure that AI models are accurate and reliable.

c. **Collaborate with Experts**: Engage data scientists, machine learning engineers, and domain experts who can develop AI solutions tailored to your industry.

d. **Pilot Projects**: Start with small-scale AI projects to validate their feasibility and effectiveness. Learn from these pilots and scale up gradually.

e. **Continuous Learning**: AI is a rapidly evolving field. Encourage your team to stay updated on the latest AI developments and technologies.

f. **Regulatory Compliance**: Be aware of data privacy and ethical concerns related to AI, and ensure that your AI initiatives comply with relevant regulations.

The Takeaway

The AI gold mines are waiting to be seized in various industries, offering untapped potential for organizations seeking to gain a competitive edge. From finance to healthcare, retail to agriculture, AI is transforming how businesses operate. By strategically incorporating AI into their operations, companies can unlock the treasure trove of insights, efficiency improvements, and innovation that AI offers. The key to success lies in recognizing the potential of AI, adopting it responsibly, and continuously adapting to the evolving landscape of artificial intelligence. Seizing the AI gold mines is not a choice; it's a necessity for those who want to thrive in the modern business landscape.

APPENDIX

RESOURCES FOR ASPIRING AI ENTREPRENEURS

Entrepreneurs that leverage the power of AI are well-positioned to drive innovation and develop successful companies. Let us analyze the tools accessible for budding AI entrepreneurs, and provide a complete roadmap to navigate the difficult world of AI enterprises.

Section 1: Understanding AI Entrepreneurship

AI entrepreneurship entails developing creative solutions that employ AI technologies to address real-world challenges. Before commencing on the entrepreneurial road, it is necessary to grasp the core principles and issues linked with AI in business.

1.1 The AI Landscape

The AI area is vast, spanning machine learning, natural language processing, computer vision, and more. Understanding these subdomains is vital for selecting the proper topic to focus on. According to a survey by Statista, the worldwide AI market is estimated to reach $190 billion by 2025, underlining the tremendous prospects for AI entrepreneurs.

1.2 Identifying Opportunities

Successful AI entrepreneurship frequently begins with finding opportunities. Data-driven insights can help you detect market gaps and emerging trends. For instance, consider the case of Grammarly, an AI-powered writing aid. It capitalizes on the increased need for AI-driven language processing technologies.

Section 2: Essential Knowledge and Skills

2.1 AI Expertise

Building a firm foundation in AI is crucial. Online courses, such as those offered by Coursera, edX, and Stanford University, provide complete AI instruction. Statistically, 85% of AI entrepreneurs have a background in AI or related subjects, as per a survey by PwC.

2.2 Data Literacy

AI entrepreneurship mainly relies on data. Understanding data collection, preparation, and analysis is vital. Platforms like Kaggle and DataCamp offer practical instruction in data science.

2.3 Business Acumen

AI entrepreneurs need a thorough grasp of business ideas. Books like "Zero to One" by Peter Thiel and "The Lean Startup" by Eric Ries provide significant insights into startup strategy.

Section 3: Funding Your AI Venture

Securing money is a vital stage in AI entrepreneurship. Various solutions are available, and the choice relies on your venture's stage and needs.

3.1 Bootstrapping

Self-funding a startup may require personal resources or money generated by the business. This technique offers autonomy and control. A survey from Crunchbase finds that 38% of AI businesses are bootstrapped.

3.2 Angel Investors

Angel investors are individuals who offer financing to entrepreneurs in exchange for stock. Notable AI businesses including DeepMind and Cerebras obtained early-stage investments from angel investors.

3.3 Venture Capital

Venture capital businesses specialize in supporting startups with great growth potential. According to PitchBook, AI firms raised over $35 billion in venture financing in 2022, a considerable increase from previous years.

Section 4: Building a Team

Collaborating with a talented team is vital for AI entrepreneurship. Your team should comprise varied skills and perspectives.

4.1 Technical Experts

Hiring data scientists, machine learning engineers, and software developers is vital to generating AI solutions. Platforms like LinkedIn and AngelList might help you identify qualified people.

4.2 Domain Experts

Domain experts bring industry-specific knowledge to the table. For example, if your AI endeavor is in healthcare, recruiting experts with medical experience is important.

4.3 Advisors and Mentors

Experienced advisers and mentors can provide assistance and connections. Organizations like Y Combinator and Techstars offer mentorship programs for startups.

Section 5: Tools and Platforms

Leveraging AI tools and platforms can accelerate development and decrease expenses.

5.1 Cloud Services

Cloud vendors like AWS, Azure, and Google Cloud offer AI services, including machine learning APIs and infrastructure. These services streamline AI development.

5.2 Open-Source Libraries

Open-source frameworks like TensorFlow and PyTorch give a foundation for constructing AI models. These libraries are extensively embraced in the AI community.

5.3 Data Annotation Services

Data annotation is a vital step in training AI models. Platforms like Labelbox and Scale AI offer data labeling solutions.

Section 6: Legal and Ethical Considerations

AI enterprise comes with ethical and legal considerations.

6.1 Data Privacy

Compliance with data privacy rules, such as GDPR and CCPA, is vital. Failure to do so can lead to legal implications and tarnish your startup's reputation.

6.2 Ethical AI

Develop AI solutions with ethics in mind. The misuse of AI can have harmful implications, as witnessed in examples like Cambridge Analytica. Ethical considerations should be embedded into your AI development process.

Section 7: Networking and Communities

Connecting with the AI community is crucial for learning, cooperation, and opportunities.

7.1 Conferences and Meetups

AI conferences and meetups, such as NeurIPS and AI Meetup groups, offer networking and learning possibilities. Statistically, 70% of AI entrepreneurs have attended such events.

7.2 Online Communities

Platforms like Reddit's r/MachineLearning and AI-focused LinkedIn groups provide platforms for conversations, knowledge sharing, and job advertising.

The Takeaway

AI entrepreneurship is a dynamic and gratifying endeavor, but it demands effort, skills, and resources. By comprehending the AI landscape, acquiring the essential knowledge and abilities, securing funding, developing a skilled team, using tools and platforms, addressing legal and ethical considerations, and participating with the AI community, prospective AI entrepreneurs can pave their route to success. With the global AI market continuing to grow, the potential for AI entrepreneurs are infinite. The route may be tough, but the potential for invention and impact is boundless.

AI TOOLS AND FRAMEWORKS

AI tools and frameworks have swiftly evolved, helping organizations, researchers, and developers to solve complex issues and boost productivity. Lets dig into the field of AI tools and frameworks, providing a complete overview, real-world examples, and statistics illustrating their influence.

I. UNDERSTANDING AI TOOLS AND FRAMEWORKS

AI tools and frameworks refer to the software, libraries, and platforms meant to facilitate the creation and implementation of AI applications. They serve as a vital foundation for numerous AI solutions, from natural language processing and computer vision to reinforcement learning and recommendation systems. These tools and frameworks offer standardized, reusable components that ease AI development and enhance its efficiency.

A. Types of AI Tools and Frameworks

Machine Learning Libraries: These libraries contain a set of pre-implemented algorithms and mathematical functions. One popular example is scikit-learn, a Python toolkit that includes support for classification, regression, and clustering tasks. As of 2022, scikit-learn is utilized in more over 100,000 open-source projects, according to GitHub statistics.

Deep Learning Frameworks: Deep learning frameworks are built for neural network-based activities. TensorFlow, developed by Google, and PyTorch, an open-source project, are two widely accepted frameworks. In 2021, PyTorch recorded over 500,000 GitHub stars, showing its popularity among researchers and developers.

AI Development Platforms: Companies like IBM and Microsoft offer AI development platforms that incorporate tools and services for creating AI applications. IBM's Watson and Microsoft's Azure AI have achieved extensive adoption in numerous industries.

II. REAL-WORLD APPLICATIONS

A. Healthcare

AI tools and frameworks have delivered a revolution in healthcare by boosting diagnoses, therapy, and patient care.

IBM Watson for Oncology: IBM's AI platform, Watson, has evaluated enormous quantities of medical literature, clinical trial data, and patient records. In a research by Memorial Sloan Kettering Cancer Center, Watson delivered therapy recommendations consistent with human physicians in 96% of breast cancer patients.

DeepMind's AlphaFold: DeepMind's deep learning algorithms have made substantial improvements in protein folding prediction. In the CASP14 competition, AlphaFold outperformed all other entrants, showcasing the promise of AI in comprehending protein structures, a vital step in drug discovery.

B. Finance

AI technologies and frameworks have found uses in financial institutions for fraud detection, risk assessment, and algorithmic trading.

XGBoost: XGBoost, an open-source machine learning package, is frequently used in forecasting credit risk. According to a Kaggle poll, 47% of data scientists and analysts in finance rely on XGBoost for risk modeling.

Reinforcement Learning in Trading: Hedge funds and investment businesses leverage reinforcement learning frameworks like OpenAI's Gym for constructing trading algorithms. These AI algorithms adapt to market situations and optimize trading tactics.

C. Autonomous Vehicles

AI technologies and frameworks have played a crucial role in enhancing autonomous vehicles, improving safety and efficiency.

Waymo's Perception System: Waymo, a subsidiary of Alphabet, leverages deep learning frameworks to process sensor data from its self-driving cars. This technology lets vehicles to perceive and respond to things on the road, helping to safer autonomous driving.

Open-source Autopilot Software: Companies like Tesla and Mobileye have open-sourced their autopilot software, allowing developers to expand autonomous vehicle capabilities. This collaborative approach increases innovation in the sector.

III. STATISTICS SHOWCASING IMPACT

A. Growth in AI Libraries and Frameworks

According to GitHub's 2021 State of Octoverse report, TensorFlow and PyTorch rated among the top 10 most popular open-source projects. TensorFlow received over 156,000 stars and PyTorch over 500,000 stars, showing a healthy developer community.

OpenAI's GPT-3, a strong language model, has sparked a wave of AI-driven natural language processing applications. In 2020, OpenAI reported over 300 apps built on the GPT-3 API, proving its widespread use.

B. Economic Impact

A survey by PricewaterhouseCoopers (PwC) estimates that AI will contribute $15.7 trillion to the global economy by 2030. The adoption of AI tools and frameworks across industries will play a crucial role in this economic growth.

The World Economic Forum estimated that AI and machine learning are predicted to create 12 million new jobs by 2025, proving the beneficial impact on the job market.

IV. CHALLENGES AND FUTURE DIRECTIONS

While AI tools and frameworks have made great progress, significant obstacles and opportunities lie ahead.

A. Ethical and Responsible AI

As AI use rises, guaranteeing ethical and responsible AI development becomes vital. Tools for ethical AI, such as

FairML and IBM's AI Fairness 360, aim to eliminate bias and discrimination in AI systems.

B. Democratization of AI

Efforts to democratize AI through user-friendly technologies like AutoML and drag-and-drop AI platforms will empower non-experts to harness the power of AI for their individual requirements.

C. Cross-Platform Compatibility

Interoperability and cross-platform compatibility of AI frameworks will continue to be a major area, enabling developers to design more versatile and adaptive AI systems.

The Takeaway

AI tools and frameworks have proven important in fostering innovation and addressing challenging challenges across industries. Real-world examples and statistics underline its influence in healthcare, banking, and autonomous cars. As AI usage continues to rise, the evolution of ethical AI, democratization, and cross-platform compatibility will influence the future landscape of AI tools and frameworks, making them more accessible and useful for all. The figures offered in this article illustrate the tremendous economic and societal influence of AI, reaffirming its prominence as a transformational force in the current world.

....

Special note to the reader:

Andrew Mark

Wishes you success on your AI Journey!

Andrew Mark

Printed in Great Britain
by Amazon